PRAISE FOR *FACT OVER FA*

"A timely revision to an essential v
Over Fake provides a concise, cogent, and insightful examination of the challenges and opportunities presented by the news media landscape of the early twenty-first century, as well as practical tools to help navigate that daunting terrain—even for those unfamiliar with, or unaccustomed to, thinking critically about how it affects their lives every day. An indispensable guide for all who aspire to think for themselves and for any conscientious citizen seeking to foster free, fairminded societies." —**Ken Stringer**, president, CommunityPlus

"People turn to news to find the truth. However, popular news, as most of us think of it, is more about perspective-making than truth-telling. So, what to do? One great start is to study Dr. Elder's excellent *Fact over Fake: A Critical Thinker's Guide to Media Bias and Political Propaganda*. Elder upholds the idea of the liberal-minded person as a fair-minded, critical thinker while simultaneously lambasting liberal and conservative ideologues who ignore intellectual autonomy and courage in support of their respective dogmas. The book provides a road map to consume news through the lens of the Paulian critical thinking framework. This work is easy to read but challenging to digest because it challenges us to look in the mirror and examine our thinking. As an educator, I am appreciative that this book contains several 'Think for Yourself' activities that are suitable for personal or group reflection. The next time you hear the phrase 'Fake News,' think carefully about who is trying to hoodwink you, and why." —**Daryl Watkins**, associate professor of organizational leadership, Embry-Riddle Aeronautical University

"*Fact over Fake* is a well-researched, scholarly, academic, and thoughtful book that is helpful in this era of misinformation, fake news, echo chambers, and information bubbles. The authors pose probing questions and provide useful lists, charts, diagrams, and graphics that readers can use as a guide. They provide a list of useful activities and questions that readers can use in their analysis of news and information. The book is a valuable and meaningful addition to works dedicated to the topics of media bias and media literacy." —**Larry Atkins**, author, *Skewed: A Critical Thinker's Guide to Media Bias*

"Paul and Elder, with their critical thinking perspective, cut into the issue of fake news, propaganda, social media dissemination and the need for professional journalism vs. social media advertisers looking for 'clicks.' The latter category focuses on 'click-bait' while the seriousness and integrity of professional journalists must be preserved. Their focus on the latest theories of consumer learning is also useful in that consumers are self-selecting news that fits their learned biases, rather than steering toward neutral sources without political bias. The fragmentation of the news market advances propaganda which is the antithesis of news. Only a critical thinking perspective on the part of news agencies and consumers can overcome the current situation, which is explained beautifully in this book." —**Myna German**, professor, mass communications, visual and performing arts, Delaware State University

"How do we become wiser consumers of the news and other information presented on the Internet, and why would this even be desirable? In this very timely book, Drs. Linda Elder and Richard Paul present a clear, comprehensive guide for those who are ready to better understand and more intelligently navigate the chaotic world of misinformation. The book begins with a review of important fundamentals, such as the concepts of news and objectivity, and discusses the powerful influences that lead to media's distortion of events. Using examples from current news stories, the guide demonstrates how the Paulian tools for critical thinking can be applied to examine the often fragmented and biased messages we receive and to skillfully analyze and evaluate their content for ourselves. Ending with an Appendix of 'Think for Yourself' exercises, this book can easily serve as a self-study companion, or a robust addition to a variety of high school and university courses." —**Agnieszka Alboszta**, American English Institute, University of Oregon

"Eye-opening, practical and thorough, this revised Thinker's Guide is required reading for today's consumer of news and media who is striving to make meaning amid the daily fray of contradictory information and shallow judgments. The clear strategies and timely insights provided in this book will enable you—as part of your regular consumption of online, print, or broadcast news—to interrogate biases, identify alternative perspectives, evaluate information and internalize the habits of a critical thinker." —**Patty Payette**, senior associate director, Delphi Center for Teaching and Learning, University of Louisville

FACT OVER FAKE

A CRITICAL THINKER'S GUIDE TO
MEDIA BIAS AND POLITICAL PROPAGANDA

RICHARD PAUL and LINDA ELDER

ROWMAN & LITTLEFIELD
Lanham • Boulder • New York • London

Acquisitions Editor: Natalie Mandziuk
Assistant Editor: Deni Remsberg
Executive Channel Manager: Karin Cholak

Credits and acknowledgments for material borrowed from other sources, and reproduced with permission, appear on the appropriate pages within the text.

Published by Rowman & Littlefield
An imprint of The Rowman & Littlefield Publishing Group, Inc.
4501 Forbes Boulevard, Suite 200, Lanham, Maryland 20706
www.rowman.com

6 Tinworth Street, London SE11 5AL, United Kingdom

British Library Cataloguing in Publication Information Available

Library of Congress Control Number: 2020943276

Library of Congress Cataloging-in-Publication Data Is Available

978-1-5381-4393-3 (cloth)
978-1-5381-4394-0 (paperback)
978-1-5381-4395-7 (electronic)

♾™ The paper used in this publication meets the minimum requirements of American National Standard for Information Sciences—Permanence of Paper for Printed Library Materials, ANSI/NISO Z39.48-1992.

This book is dedicated to the life and professional contributions of Edward R. Murrow (1908–1965), a distinguished journalist whose name symbolizes intellectual courage, intellectual integrity, and the pursuit of truth in the news. Here are some of his thoughts, which media outlets essentially ignored during his lifetime and which are still chiefly disregarded:

> This [radio] program is not a place where personal opinion should be mixed up with ascertainable facts. . . . It is not, I think, humanly possible for any reporter to be completely objective, for we are all to some degree prisoners of our education, travel, reading—the sum total of our experience.

> Everyone is a prisoner of his own experiences. No one can eliminate prejudices—just recognize them.

> One of the basic troubles with radio and television news is that both instruments have grown up as an incompatible combination of show business, advertising and news. Each of the three is a rather bizarre and demanding profession. . . . The top management of the networks with a few notable exceptions, has been trained in advertising, research, sales or show business. But by the nature of the corporate structure, they also make the final and crucial decisions having to do with news and public affairs. Frequently they have neither the time nor the competence to do this.

> Just once in a while let us exalt the importance of ideas and information.

CONTENTS

INTRODUCTION

Why Critical Thinking Is Essential to Making Sense of the News

Since our first edition of this publication, released just over ten years ago, the concept of *news media* has profoundly expanded. At that time, "news media" fundamentally referred to what would then have been considered mainstream news sources, specifically newspapers, magazines, and TV news. Today, with the explosion of the internet, the concept of the "news" perhaps more accurately represents every individual website through which "news" of any kind is propagated, along with traditional mainstream news sources. This would include the millions of personal web pages in which news is given out publicly, or even in private groups, on a daily basis.

The news comes to us, then, not only from professional journalists, many of whom embrace ethical principles. It also comes from unprofessional journalists who deliberately slant, distort, and misrepresent the news. And it comes from people who spread false representations

> To what degree and how is "the news," as presented by a given news outlet, affected by politics and the political climate?

of the news (some who are well-meaning but naïve). We now get our news online, from TV and radio, as well as in print. We find news in traditional articles as well as op-eds and commentary, social media echo chambers, and late-night shows that target the news for comedy.

Though the number of sources now included under the umbrella of *news media* has expanded exponentially in the past decade, in this book we will use the term "news media" to refer to established news organizations, rather than tackling the broader concept of the news as coming from individual persons and websites.

Though some essential features of the news have changed dramatically in the past decade or more, *the basic logic of news media has not changed*. Indeed, the logic behind bias and propaganda in the news media is simple, and it is the same the world over. Each society, culture, and group has a distinctive worldview. This worldview colors what we see within a given culture or group, and how we see it. News media in the cultures and subcultures of the world reflect the worldview of each culture, or group, for which they write. But the truth of what is happening in the world is far more complicated than what appears to be true within any group.

To think critically about "the news," one must come to terms with this truth and think about the news using explicit tools of critical thinking.

Unfortunately, the term "critical thinking" has been inappropriately commandeered on both sides of the political spectrum in the United States, with significant implications for how one perceives the news in our country. Conservatives see themselves as thinking critically and advancing a critical thinking agenda, while "postmodern liberals"[1] see themselves as the critical thinkers. In fact, critical thinking doesn't belong to any group, nor is it entrenched in any ideology. Instead, critical thinking, properly perceived, offers objective tools of analysis and assessment that enable us to see through propaganda and distortions of thought on any part of the political spectrum and in any part of the news. Critical thinkers are not held hostage by any schools of thought or belief systems, but rather seek to impartially assess all thoughts and actions according to intellectual standards such as *accuracy*, *relevance*, *logic*, *significance*, *depth*, *breadth*, *sufficiency*, and *fairness*. Those who aspire to criticality do not feel the need to align themselves with group dogmas, but instead attempt at all times to embody intellectual autonomy and intellectual courage in thinking through issues in the news and elsewhere.

Many so-called critical thinking guides to media bias in the United States are written from a political point of view (usually that of the Republican or Democratic Party). Sometimes authors will make clear their political positions, while others veil their political opinions. Our goal in this book is not to take a political position, though we do occasionally use examples that may appear political in order to prove a conceptual point. We try to avoid assuming any political position precisely because what is *most important is that people learn the tools of critical thinking,* and the principles deriving from them,

> Do the owners of this news outlet hold a particular political position? If so, how do their political views influence how they present the news?

rather than focusing on a given critique of a given political issue and becoming distracted by one's associations or emotions around that issue. This is important, again, because people on either side, or at any point, on the political spectrum may think more or less critically about a given issue, and we do not want any example we give to lead you to stereotype us as conservatives, liberals, or belonging to some other political category. In most cases, rather than giving examples to support a given point, we usually ask you to identify examples of your own (through activities in Appendix A). In so doing, you should either come to see the power in what we are saying, or decide that our theory is not sound. It is up to you as an intellectually autonomous thinker, employing freedom of thought and critical reflection, to make these, and indeed all, decisions about which ideas to accept and which to reject.

---

1   We use here the term "post-modern" liberal, since the term liberal has been altered from its original, and more appropriate uses, and is often equated with the Democratic Party. Although the Democratic Party does entail some liberal features, it falls short of embracing the classic liberally educated mind. For more on this, see our section *Political Views in the News: Understanding the Liberal-Minded Person*.

In line with this point, as you attempt to make sense of the news, your focus should be more on the *reasoning* of news reporters, politicians, or indeed anyone, rather than on the specific position they are taking. Again, people can think critically or uncritically, as a matter of degree, across the political spectrum, with some notable exceptions. Your challenge is to carefully examine the reasoning embedded in a news story and *judge the story by the soundness of that reasoning*, setting aside where the reasoning falls on the political spectrum.

Critical thinking is a complex set of skills that reverses what is unreasonable, but natural and instinctive, in human thought. On the other hand, news coverage in a society tends to operate with the following maxims:

- "This is how it appears to us from our point of view; therefore, this is the way it is."
- "These are the facts that support our way of looking at this; therefore, these are the most important facts."
- "These countries or groups are friendly to us; therefore, they deserve praise."
- "These countries or groups are unfriendly to us; therefore, they deserve criticism and even punishment."
- "These are the stories most interesting or sensational to our readers; therefore, these are the most important stories in the news."

Critical readers reverse each of these maxims. They actively use tools of criticality to understand the news, to glean from the news what is sound and discard what is unsound, with the goal of developing a reasonable view of what is actually happening in the world without bias or prejudice.

Again, in Appendix A you will find "Think for Yourself" activities that invite you to put into action the theory we introduce. These will be referred to throughout the book. Of course, you may choose to do the suggested activity after a given section, or at any time. However, we hope you do not perceive these activities as "add-ons," and therefore something that can be skipped. Rather, we hope you recognize that it is precisely when you apply theory to something of importance (to you) that it takes root in your thinking and begins to elevate you to higher levels of thought and action. Reading and simultaneously agreeing or disagreeing with a given point will not transform the way you think about media bias and political propaganda in the news. Applying powerful truths about media bias and proceeding with caution and critical reasoning when ingesting the news will. Our activities are designed to support and advance this process in your thinking.

WHAT IS NEWS?

There is a sense in which "news" may be considered a form of history. History focuses on events of the past; similarly, news refers to a circumstance or set of circumstances occurring in the past; "the news," as presented to us in various forms, captures how we tell the history of yesterday or even a few minutes ago. While the term "news" typically refers to the reporting of a recent past event or set of events, history typically refers to "the narration, representation, or study of events or phenomena."[2] One important difference between news and history is that history tends to focus on a clustering of events over some spread of time that includes a historical narrative entailing interpretations of events. We might say that news is a very brief view of the history of yesterday, or again, of even a few minutes ago. When people gossip, they are telling "news" as they understand it, however trivial, and they are engaging in a form of historical thinking, however shallow and unworthy.

Another important difference between news and history is that history tends to take a longer view into the past than does the news, is expected to be well-researched over a period of time, should better deal with complexities within the issues being studied than does the typical news outlet, and if well-reasoned, will illuminate sociocentric and egocentric patterns of living in the past that should be avoided by humans in the future. Historians have differing purposes than do news reporters and outlets, and tend to be less bridled by economic constraints. They are expected to use discerning judgment and therefore not to pander to any side of a political position, while news reporters often now see their primary role as taking a political position rather than remaining objective. And the populace seems largely to agree, since news consumers increasingly frequent news outlets that

> To what degree is the news affected by the wishes and motives of advertisers that largely pay for the news?

take advocacy positions. Historians more openly critique customs, taboos, and more than do news reporters. In studying, reporting and interpreting the past, historians can more readily reveal dysfunctionality within societies than can the news media, since, by peering back in time, historians can more objectively assess human traditions. In other words, the further away from traditions and behaviors we are in time, the easier it is to accurately and logically assess them, on the whole. On the other hand, typical news reporters, themselves situated within and usually entrenched in the taboos, customs, and traditions of society, cannot be expected to accurately and logically critique current customs. Of course, there are exceptions. Be on the lookout for these in the news.

People seem to have an innate need to tell themselves stories of the past, both as news and as history, given that we have been doing so since before the beginning of recorded history. The extent to which the stories we tell ourselves about either the recent or distant past are sound and worthy of our attention entirely depends upon the reasoning of the people telling those stories. Some say we study the past to learn what

---

2   Definition taken from *Oxford English Dictionary* (OED.com, 2019).

to avoid in the future. But if so, either we aren't studying the past, or we are not taking seriously the lessons we are "studying" in our stories, those of yesterday or long ago.

POLITICAL VIEWS IN THE NEWS: UNDERSTANDING THE LIBERAL-MINDED PERSON

In reading the news it is important to understand something of how people tend to be categorized politically in today's climate, since these groups rally around opposing news outlets. From the viewpoint of political orientation, people in the United States are characteristically categorized, if at all, as either "conservative," typically connected with the Republican Party, or "liberal," usually associated with the Democratic Party. But neither of the two pairings tell the full picture; and this way of looking at politics may grossly misrepresent people who do not identify as either Democrats or Republicans but still think of themselves as liberal or conservative, or having inclinations toward both ends of the political spectrum on different issues. In other words, conservative or liberal positions should be understood in terms of a continuum, rather than in terms of black and white, in which a person may move from right to left or left to right depending on the issue. For instance, people frequently want big government for one set of goals, and small government for another set of goals. Big government is now considered a "liberal" position, while small government is considered "conservative," but again, a liberal person may for the most part prefer small government (as has been the case historically) and a more conservative person may sometimes opt for larger government. In short, a person can hold both traditionally conservative views on some issues, while holding a more traditionally liberal position on other issues. In other words, to say of a man that he is conservative, properly speaking, is not to say that he is necessarily of the Republican Party, but rather that he has conservative views on many or most issues. At the same time, to say of a woman that she is liberal is not necessarily to imply that she is a Democrat or never appreciates or takes a conservative position. Yet the news media treat people as if we all neatly fit into these two narrow and frequently improper categories of "conservative" (i.e., Republican), or "liberal" (i.e., Democrat).

One good way to avoid these labels is to begin with a rich idea of the *liberal-minded person*, which should not be equated with any given political party in the United States today. The concept of the liberal mind relates with the concept of *liberal education*, which entails fairminded critical thinking, intellectual cultivation, emancipation of the mind, and the advancement of freedom of thought, along with the protection of all inalienable human rights. Cultivating the liberally educated mind is rarely the focus of higher education today, which is instead run largely according to business principles and values and preparing people for the "work world." A liberal-minded person embodies intellectual virtues such as intellectual autonomy, intellectual integrity, intellectual humility, intellectual empathy, and confidence in reasoning. Liberal-minded persons think through every political issue from the point of reasonability and ethical responsibility. They are not beholden to any political party because they recognize potential strengths and weaknesses in most political parties.

It is helpful to consider how educated persons use the term "liberal," which we should be able to find in a good dictionary. The *Oxford English Dictionary* (OED online, 2019) gives this definition: "free from bias, prejudice, or bigotry; open-minded, tolerant . . . favoring social reform and a degree of state intervention in matters of economics and social justice . . . directed to a general broadening of the mind . . . open to the reception of new ideas or proposals of reform . . . supporting or advocating individual rights, civil liberties, and political and social reform tending towards individual freedom or democracy with little state intervention."

To the degree that any political party embodies these principles, it can be said to be liberal in orientation. But if the term "liberal" is commandeered by people who do not understand its meaning, political correctness can and does result. When this happens, the political party claiming to be liberal, rather than advocating open-mindedness, the pursuit of equal rights and the advancement of freedoms, instead advances, perhaps inadvertently, the narrowing of freedoms in accord with their own political views. For instance, all reasonable persons will agree that sexual harassment should be denounced and avoided. But sometimes what appears to one as sexual harassment may instead entail simply approaching a person one is attracted to and giving that person unwanted attention that then must be pointed out. An off-color joke or remark today can mean the end of someone's career. In the workplace, many people do not think it appropriate for people of different genders to have professional meetings alone, without others present, as if they needed a chaperone to ensure neither party becomes flirtatious or makes an unwanted advance. For instance, the *New York Times* reports that, according to one of their polls, around 25 percent of those polled believe that "private work meetings with colleagues of the opposite sex are inappropriate. Nearly two-thirds say people should take extra caution around members of the opposite sex at work."[3] Any sort of physical contact at all is now all but banned in the workplace, so that simply lightly touching someone's arm can result in a sexual harassment claim. If a student is made to feel "uncomfortable" in the classroom, the professor may lose her or his job, even when that discomfort comes simply from the normal

> To what degree is news being given to the people according to what they want to hear, rather than what they would rather not know or have to face?

---

3   Miller, C. (July 1, 2017). "It's Not Just Mike Pence: Americans Are Wary of Being Alone with the Opposite Sex." *New York Times*. https://www.nytimes.com/2017/07/01/upshot/members-of-the-opposite-sex-at-work-gender-study.html.

confusion, perplexity, and uneasiness that accompanies any form of deep and transformative learning (which is the primary purpose of education).

Vulgar, unsophisticated, and overly simplistic views should never be confused with critical, high-minded thought, nor with a liberal viewpoint; yet these and related positions are often pushed by those who consider themselves "left-leaning." Similarly, conservative viewpoints should not automatically be stereotyped as "right-leaning" or Republican. Of course, many liberal-minded persons and conservative critical thinkers choose to affiliate with political parties outside of the Democratic or Republican Party. Or they stand alone without allegiance to any political party, taking each issue as it comes, making the best judgments based on the evidence and other essential tools of criticality. They actively seek well-thought-through news stories, in both mainstream and alternative news sources.

THE LOGIC OF THE NEWS MEDIA

The logic of the news media is both simple and complex. On the one hand, many reporters see themselves as objectively informing the public of important information—and in many cases, this is precisely what they are doing. Yet, on the other hand, it seems that reporters themselves do not have a shared conception of objectivity in the news. Indeed, the *Society for Professional Journalism* has recently removed the term "objectivity" from its list of primary purposes because the term now apparently means different things to different journalists (Atkins, 2016). One might then ask: how can the news be objective when reporters themselves have neither a shared understanding of the very term "objective," nor feel the need even to aspire to it in their work?

POLITICAL INFLUENCES, ADVERTISING, AND GROUP THINK

The lack of a shared concept of "objectivity" on the part of journalists reveals that reporting the news is not so straightforward as it usually appears and is presented. Yet there is an overarching logic underlying the news of which critical news consumers are well aware, and which is the primary focus of this book. For instance, you cannot critically examine the news without understanding the connection between politics and news coverage, because political parties often have deep affiliations with major news outlets—increasingly so as advocacy journalism has become more the norm than an anomaly in recent times. Indeed, some news outlets are flagrant voices for a given political party, without demur nor apparent need to explain their political biases. (To deepen your understanding of this problem, work through *Think for Yourself 1: Targeting Political Journalism* in Appendix A.)

Just as politics plays a major role in media bias, so also does money, since politics and money typically go hand in hand. Political forces and advertisers influence media content in ways frequently hidden from the news consumer. Consequently, to understand the logic of the news media is to understand, as a beginning place, the logic of the relationships between the news media, politics, and economics (or, in other words, money).

Another key variable in grasping the logic of the news entails understanding sociocentric biases, or group think, and how group biases affect the news as it is disseminated to the people—including the fact that people fundamentally want to agree with the news and therefore seek news outlets that validate their own biases, prejudices, and worldviews. In other words, because the news must be sold to the people, naturally it must be palatable to its audience. Consequently, news outlets typically give their audiences what they want to hear and will naturally agree with. Clearly this is not in line with critical thinking or objectively discerning what is happening in the world.

_____

What news outlets should I rely on?

_____

Whenever you seek the news from one or more outlets, you might therefore ask:

- To what degree and how is "the news," as presented by this outlet, affected by politics and the political climate? (Politics)
- Do the owners of this news outlet hold a particular political position, and if so, how might their political views and affiliations influence the ways in which "news" is disseminated through this outlet? (Politics)
- To what degree is the news affected by the wishes and motives of advertisers that largely pay for the news? How can this even be determined? (Money)
- To what degree is news being given to the people in accordance with what they want or like to hear, rather than making them uncomfortable by telling them news they would rather not know or have to face? (Sociocentrism or groupthink)

TECHNOLOGICAL NOISE IN THE NEWS

Adding to these complexities, current trends in technology have radically changed the way we experience the news. Through their questions, critical thinkers examine how these complexities affect the way they receive, pursue, and interpret the news. For instance, they might ask:

- How is my ability to think deeply about complex issues presented in the news being affected by the constant bombardment of advertisements from companies strictly targeting me, increasing the likelihood that I will be highly distracted by those ads (precisely because they are designed to appeal specifically to me)? In other words, how does this barrage of personal ads affect my ability to read and reasonably interpret the news across different platforms? *(We now have ad blocking software that can be downloaded to cut down on some of this noise.)*

- If I'm reading all of my news on a small device like a cell phone, how do I experience the news differently from when I can see it on a larger page such as a magazine, newspaper, or even a larger computer screen? How can I even know how this is affecting my ability to reasonably interpret the news?

In the end, it is up to each of us to ask these questions as well:

- What news outlets should I pursue? What criteria am I using to make this decision?
- Do my biases lead me toward certain news outlets and away from others?
- How can I find reputable alternative news sources?
- Am I even open to considering alternative, perhaps more reasonable, ways of looking at the news?

WHAT WE NEED THE NEWS MEDIA TO DO FOR US

As readers of the news, we are often caught up in following news stories as if they came to us from on high—as if these were the only stories worth knowing, since they are the ones given to us by whichever particular news outlets we choose to follow. But when we look closely at what passes for news, we may wonder whether more important or enlightening stories are being ignored, and whether we are wasting our time, or being misled, by the stories we read. What we need the news media to do, among other important things, is:

1. Illuminate best practices throughout human societies in potentially every important domain of human thought.
2. Focus on what is most significant in advancing human life and wellbeing, rather than highlighting and propagating the trivial.
3. Enlighten and educate us.
4. Point out the most pressing problems we humans face, including our treatment of one another, other sentient creatures, and our home—planet earth.
5. Illuminate problems from all reasonable significant perspectives, without fearing that news consumers may take a position contrary to the "party line" or the status quo.
6. Offer real investigative journalism that uncovers issues which should be of concern to us.

Critical consumers of the news are aware of the inherent weaknesses in the logic of news media largely controlled by money, political power, and groupthink. They therefore seek ways, through alternative news sources, to counter biased mainstream news. And they have a broader historical perspective of the news, with a keen awareness of how news stories today fit into broader historical patterns of human ideas and actions.

CHAPTER 1

CURRENT TRENDS AFFECTING HOW WE SEE THE NEWS

Our primary goal in this book is to lay out central concepts and principles in critical thinking that all people need if they are to effectively think their way through the news, weeding out the mass of media bias and propaganda along the way. Before delving into these concepts and principles in Chapter 2, we can suggest some further critical thinking questions you can immediately employ to uncover media bias and political propaganda in the news.

KEY CRITICAL THINKING QUESTIONS TO ASK WHEN SEEKING THE NEWS

- Is this news source reputable? In other words: Does it appear to at least attempt to present the news in an unbiased manner? Does it have a track record of reporting actual stories, rather than urban myths, conspiracy theories, and other unfounded claims?

- Does this news source openly publish retractions and corrections after making errors in its reporting?

- Where do these reporters get their information? What additional sources do they use to corroborate their information? Are they or their editors paid to run a story, or are they paid not to run a story?

- Is this news source merely a gossip column, a political smear organization, or some other dysfunctional information source with an unsavory agenda? If so, why would I waste my time with, and potentially be led astray by, these sources? (Realize that it is easy to be influenced by irrational thinking merely through exposure, even when you think you are guarding against it).

> Is this news source reputable? Does it present the news in an unbiased manner? Does it have a track record of reporting actual stories, rather than urban myths, conspiracy theories, and other unfounded claims?

- What is the purpose of this news outlet? Is the purpose clearly stated? Is there a hidden agenda? If so, how can I identify that agenda?

- Do professional journalists write for this news outlet? What are the credentials of these journalists?

- Am I seeking news on websites such as social media sites? If so, do I realize I'm getting the news filtered to me, often through unreliable sources? (Bottom line: *avoid getting news from any social media sites* since you would have to work doubly hard to assess the "news" found there—and who has the time?)

- Does this news source attempt at all to enlighten people, or does it merely pander to the views of consumers by maintaining the status quo?

- To what degree is sensationalism a goal of this news source? Why am I drawn to sensationalism, scandal, and melodrama?

These questions can help you focus on the most reputable news sources, which is an essential starting place. Even then, you should never read the news without using skills of criticality, since problems are potentially inherent in any and all news sources, however "reputable." This should become clearer as you read on.

REALITIES THAT IMPEDE OUR ABILITY TO GET OBJECTIVE NEWS

In the past decade, with the explosion of the internet and its attendant realities, it has become increasingly difficult to get objective news (and it was difficult even before this explosion). Many of these realities are now being documented in articles and books, though none of us can keep up with them, so rapid are these changes. We therefore do not attempt to address them all, but rather touch upon several that are important.[1]

Here, then, are a few of the most powerful trends now facing consumers of news:

1. It is now very easy to find enclaves of specialized (and biased) news outlets, and social media news-related threads or webpages, that fit one's own worldview and presuppositions. News consumers can therefore effortlessly find news sources in keeping with their preconceived notions of the world, and can connect with people of like mind, however distorted their collective views may be. Through these news sources, their biases are collectively validated, enabling them to incorporate news stories (however inaccurate or misleading) into their worldview based on how the stories make them feel—that is, how well these stories fit into their existing views, how much they wish the claims were true, or how well the stories fit the views of their friends and colleagues. These consumers seem to rarely corroborate news reports on their own. They rarely or never seek out the same stories as reported by other sources, where the stories may be reported with a broader context, or with more details or with emphasis on different elements.

---

1   See our Recommended Readings list at the back of this book for several publications that take you deeper into current trends in the news and related topics.

Consequently, these news consumers are able to keep their biased views intact, and thereby avoid facing objective reality.

2. Indeed, many people get their "news" solely from free-for-all social media websites *that adhere to no standards of reasonability*, and which are hodgepodges of poorly reasoned and well-reasoned thoughts and ideas mixed together in ways that cannot delineate to the consumer which "news" is reputable. On the other hand, many well-meaning people try to critique and even investigate what appear to be biased news sources, but, lacking critical thinking skills, they are unclear how to do so.

3. With the decline of newspaper circulation has come the rise of advocacy journalism, in which many news outlets now actively take positions on the news as if the primary purpose were to editorialize rather than simply report the news in its most objective form. This phenomenon can be found across the political spectrum, from conservative to post-modern liberal journalism—whether moderate, far-right, or far-left. And people are now flocking and clustering to these advocacy news outlets. Larry Atkins (2016), in his book *Skewed*, reports, "On May 28, 2014, Fox News marked its 149th

> Where do these reporters get their information? What additional sources do they use to corroborate their information? Are they or their editors paid to run a story, or are they paid not to run a story?

consecutive month as the most-watched cable news network, beating MSNBC and CNN combined in total viewers and ranking sixth among all ad-supported cable networks in both total daytime and primetime audience size" (p. 9). Fox news is an advocacy political news organization primarily focused on advancing a Republican agenda.

Atkins gives this example of how advocacy journalism plays itself out in the news every day:

> Whenever there is a mass shooting in the United States, liberal media outlets like the *New York Times* editorial page, MSNBC hosts Rachel Maddow and Lawrence O'Donnell, and liberal websites like *Salon* will push the discussion to advocate for more gun-control. In contrast, conservative media pundits like FOX News hosts Sean Hannity and Tucker Carlson, and talk radio hosts like Rush Limbaugh and Mark Levine will staunchly defend the Second Amendment right to bear arms and vehemently oppose any type of regulation. (p. 11)

4. Of course, all advocacy journalism is not of the same quality. Whether and to what degree a position should be taken in journalism entirely depends on the case at hand and the arguments being given. In the final analysis, each of us must use our critical thinking abilities to determine the best position to take

on an issue, once we are informed of all reasonable sides. We must be open to considering all rational perspectives on an issue, the complexities of which should be reflected in news reporting.

5. Perhaps surprisingly, many people are still unaware of the prevalence of fake news throughout social media and the web. It is now well-known that people and organizations (including private interest groups, businesses, and governments) can create authentic-looking websites[2] featuring deliberately misleading or utterly fabricated stories. Fake news can spread quickly through social media, and a fake story can become "common knowledge" amongst a large segment of the population in a matter of days. One example is the Pizzagate conspiracy theory that went viral during the 2016 U.S. presidential campaign, in which the email account of John Podesta, Hillary Clinton's campaign manager, was hacked. Conspiracy theorists claimed that the emails entailed coded messages connecting several U.S. restaurants and high-ranking officials of the Democratic Party with purported human trafficking and a child sex ring. These unfounded claims went viral, spreading through the use of several social media sites (including Twitter and Facebook), among ultra-conservatives and other groups antagonistic to Clinton or the Democratic Party.[3]

6. Many people are unable to distinguish between news stories and news commentary. These people are therefore unaware that a news story should not entail judgment on the part of the story's author, but rather should simply report accurate, verifiable, undistorted information, or in other words *facts*. News commentary, on the other hand, involves taking a position on an issue and therefore may be well or poorly reasoned. When news reporters do editorialize, they should make it clear when they are presenting facts versus when they are suggesting their inferences or conclusions based on the facts.

7. Many people get their news from news-based comedy programs—television and internet broadcasts whose purpose is to make people laugh by focusing on current events. This can include sketches with exaggerated or otherwise altered versions of events (e.g., *Saturday Night Live*), as well as comedic commentary on current news (e.g., *The Daily Show*). Of course, such shows have financial incentives to prioritize comedy above unbiased and even-handed delivery of objective information. At the same time, comedy writers often voice, through wit, their own views on politics and the news, and hence their "jokes" are frequently intended to, and frequently do, influence consumers' views.

---

2 For a list of examples, see https://en.wikipedia.org/wiki/List_of_fake_news_websites. See also: https://www.nytimes.com/2019/10/31/upshot/fake-local-news.html?action=click&module =News&pgtype=Homepage.

3 For more on this, see https://www.nytimes.com/2016/12/05/business/media/comet-ping-pong-pizza -shooting-fake-news-consequences.html?searchResultPosition=1.

THE PROBLEM OF FAKE NEWS

Though the problem of fake news—the actual and deliberate distribution of false information—is real enough (and now widely documented), the term "fake news" is frequently misused to reference stories a person or group dislikes, or information reported in the news they wish were not true. Fake news typically refers to the intentional spreading of fabrications and false information through digital sources.

The history of the term "fake news" can be traced to ancient times, since, as Barclay (2018) has pointed out, "fake news is really just the latest name for the ancient art of lying." But the term has become widespread in the twenty-first century with the digital information explosion. One improper but widespread use of "fake news" refers to the desire of some political groups, and related news outlets, to avoid facing information that *is in fact true.* Through a commonly used psychological defense mechanism known as *projection,* a person or group attributes to another person or group what they themselves are thinking or feeling, in order to avoid their own unacceptable thoughts and feelings.[4] Put in simpler terms, this is the tactic: *accuse your opponent of doing what he or she is accusing you of doing.*[5] For instance, some well-known radical and reactionary political news pundits and groups continually accuse more honest media outlets of spreading "fake news" while they themselves are the ones initiating and disseminating fake news. This allows the dishonest journalists and news agencies to disguise their fraudulence while simultaneously taking an offensive position. In so doing, they are able to hoodwink their followers and recruit even more naïve thinkers into their political camp. (To deepen your understanding of this problem, work through *Think for Yourself 2: Identify Accusations of Spreading Fake News* in Appendix A.)

> Is this news source merely a gossip column, a smear organization, or some other dysfunctional information source with an unsavory agenda?

SOCIAL MEDIA AS AN UNRELIABLE NEWS SOURCE

Though, as we have already pointed out, social media is a poor vehicle for getting the news, the Pew Research Center reports that 62 percent of U.S. adults now say they get news through social media websites.[6]

4　This and other defense mechanisms were illuminated and developed by Sigmund and Anna Freud. For more on the pathologies of the human mind, see *The Thinker's Guide to the Human Mind: Thinking, Feeling, Wanting, and the Problem of Irrationality, Fourth Edition,* by Linda Elder and Richard Paul (Lanham, MD: Rowman & Littlefield, reprint edition 2019).

5　For more on fallacies in thought, see *The Thinker's Guide to Fallacies: The Art of Mental Trickery and Manipulation: 44 Foul Ways to Win an Argument,* by Richard Paul and Linda Elder (Lanham, MD: Rowman & Littlefield, reprint edition 2019).

6　See: https://www.journalism.org/2016/05/26/news-use-across-social-media-platforms-2016/.

News consumers are frequently misled by one or more of these means via social media websites:

- The paid placement of fake or misleading news. For instance, in October of 2019, Facebook CEO Mark Zuckerberg admitted to allowing politicians to lie through paid advertisements on Facebook (the leading social network site).
- The sharing of fake or misleading news, both by malicious and naïve parties.
- The sharing of real news accompanied by the sharer's commentary, where consumers read the commentary (however inaccurate or misleading it may be) rather than the story itself, and therefore come away with an erroneous idea of what the story reports.
- The sharing of real news where people only read the headline or synopsis, and therefore don't understand the context or nuances of the story, or how the story might appear from a different viewpoint.
- The sharing of news commentary, which, again, many people mistake for objective news reporting.[7]
- Their own false assumption that the news found through social media is to be considered just as valid and reliable as news generated by reputable nonpartisan sources.

What is the purpose of this news outlet? Is the purpose clearly stated? Is there a hidden agenda? If so, how can I identify that agenda?

While propagating false or misleading ideas certainly happens beyond the confines of social media, the nature of social media (designed to keep users scrolling and shallowly engaged through repeated, addictive dopamine spikes) increases the likelihood of people becoming and remaining misinformed.

---

7   See: https://www.americanpressinstitute.org/publications/reports/survey-research/americans-and-the -news-media/.

CHAPTER 2

ESSENTIAL CRITICAL THINKING TOOLS FOR UNDERSTANDING HUMAN REASONING AND MEDIA LOGIC

People tend to approach the news primarily through their own prejudicial and biased lenses. For these people, thinking critically about the news is chiefly out of reach. However, when writing this book we began with the assumption that our readers (YOU) are concerned with seeing the world as it is, which means, among other things, fully understanding and confidently facing objective reality, rather than mechanically following a given ideological path (however well-worn). We also assume that our readers value fairmindedness in their daily thought and actions, for without an orientation toward fairmindedness and other intellectual virtues such as intellectual empathy, intellectual humility, confidence in reason, and intellectual integrity, one cannot hope to see through media bias and propaganda.

In this chapter we delineate foundational tools of critical thinking that will help the discerning and judicious thinker reason more critically about anything and everything that now falls under the heading of "the news." We outline the basic concepts and principles in a rich conception of critical thinking, and we offer some brief contextualizations to media logic. In later chapters we further contextualize these foundational concepts to help you better understand and decipher the news, and to help you ward off manipulation by unethical politicians and their caravans of news pundits.

> Is the article, editorial, or story clear?

When you internalize the tools of critical thinking, you should reason at a higher level about the news, *as well as throughout all parts of your life*. This follows from the fact that *all of the news comes from reasoning*; when we understand reasoning and everything it entails, we are better able to judge any and all reasoning, of which the news is only one type. In other words, the principles of critical thinking apply across all domains of human life, and these principles are the same, no matter the content. Understanding media logic is only one domain of thought for which critical reasoning is essential if we are not to be manipulated and hoodwinked.

DEFINING CRITICAL THINKING

It is helpful to begin with a brief definition of critical thinking, though there are many ways to articulate the concept within a range. Here is one definition:

> Everyone thinks; it is our nature to do so. But much of our thinking, left to itself, is biased, distorted, partial, uninformed, or downright prejudiced. Yet the quality of our life and of what we produce, make, or build depends precisely on the quality of our thought. Poor thinking takes a tremendous toll on the quality of life. If we want to think well, we must understand at least the rudiments of thought, the most basic structures out of which all thinking is made. In other words, we must learn how to deconstruct reasoning in order to examine its parts. Once deconstructed, we then need to assess the reasoning for quality. Further, we must actively work toward embodying intellectual characteristics or virtues as a way of life. This entails understanding and combatting our native human tendencies toward egocentric and sociocentric thought, both of which stand as formidable barriers to the cultivation of ethical critical reasoning.

A Comprehensive Approach to Critical Thinking

Critical thinking entails the disciplined analysis and assessment of reasoning as one cultivates intellectual virtues. This process includes concern for two primary barriers to criticality—egocentric and sociocentric thinking—which are prevalent and widespread in human thought and life. Media bias and propaganda arise from these pathologies.

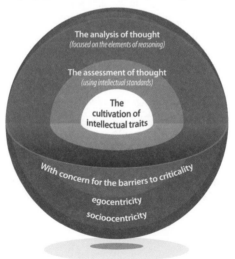

The analysis of thought
(focused on the elements of reasoning)

The assessment of thought
(using intellectual standards)

The cultivation of intellectual traits

With concern for the barriers to criticality

egocentricity

socioocentricity

ALL HUMANS USE THEIR THINKING
TO MAKE SENSE OF THE WORLD

The words "thinking" and "reasoning" are used in everyday life as virtual synonyms (as we typically use them in our writing). However, reasoning is more specific, because it highlights the inference-drawing capacity of the mind and focuses on issues, problems, and questions to be reasoned through.

Reasoning occurs whenever the mind draws conclusions on the basis of reasons. We draw conclusions whenever we make sense of things. Usually, we are not aware of the full scope of reasoning implicit in our minds.

We begin to reason from the moment we wake up in the morning. We reason when we figure out what to eat for breakfast, what to wear, whether to make certain purchases, or whether to go with this or that friend to lunch. We reason as we interpret the oncoming flow of traffic, when we react to the decisions of other drivers, or when we speed up or slow down. One can draw conclusions, then, about everyday events or, really, about anything at all: about poems, microbes, people, numbers, historical events, social settings, psychological states, character traits, the past, the present, the future, and so on.

> If I accept the line of reasoning being presented in the article, what implications or consequences are likely? If I ignore the line of reasoning being presented in the article, what implications or consequences are likely?

By reasoning, then, we refer to making sense of something by giving it some meaning in our minds. Virtually all thinking is part of our sense-making activities. We hear scratching at the door and think, "It's the dog." We see dark clouds in the sky and think, "It looks like rain." Some of this activity operates at a subconscious level. For example, all of the sights and sounds about us have meaning to us without our explicitly noticing them.

When we read, see, or hear news, we must use our reasoning to make sense of it or, in other words, draw proper inferences from it. And we must understand all "news" as *products* of one or more person's reasoning. It is only *through our reasoning* that we can understand the reasoning embedded in the news. To do this requires that we grasp what is entailed in reasoning itself.

On the surface, reasoning often looks as if it has no component structures. Examined more closely, however, it implies the ability to engage in a set of interrelated intellectual processes. Learning these structures will enable you to better understand what is going on beneath the surface of what you read, what you hear, and what you see in the news.

ANALYZE THINKING THROUGH ITS ELEMENTAL STRUCTURES

Eight basic structures are present in all thinking. Whenever we think, we think for a purpose, within a point of view, based on assumptions, leading to implications and consequences. We use concepts, ideas, and theories to interpret data, facts, and experiences in order to answer questions, solve problems, and resolve issues.

Thinking, then:

- generates purposes

- raises questions

- uses information

- utilizes concepts

- makes inferences

- makes assumptions

- generates implications

- embodies a point of view

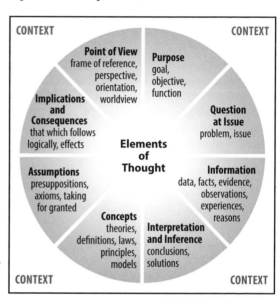

Each of these structures has implications for the others. If your purposes or goals change, so do the related questions and problems. If the questions or problems important to you change, you are then forced to seek new information and data. If you begin to question certain assumptions in your thinking, you may see information (e.g., in the news) in a different light, and so on. Every news story derives from these elements of thought and should be analyzed accordingly.

How can I check the information in this news story or editorial?

To Analyze Thinking We Must Learn to Identify and Question Its Elemental Structures

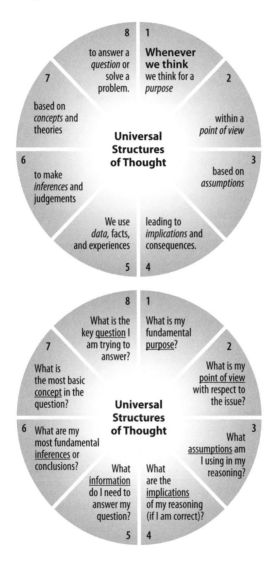

Be aware: When we understand the structures of thought, we ask important questions implied by these structures as we read the "news."

QUESTIONING THE REASONING EMBEDDED IN A NEWS ARTICLE

To analyze the news we must learn to identify and question our own reasoning as well as the reasoning embedded in the news. Question the reasoning embedded in news articles with these prompts:

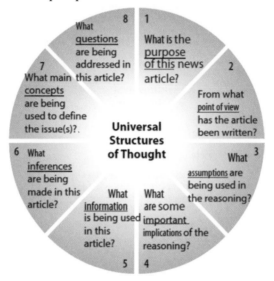

Question your own reasoning while reading the news using these questions as guides:

Reason Through News Articles, Editorials and Stories—A Checklist

All news articles have a PURPOSE.

1. Is the purpose of the news article clear, or is the purpose muddled, vague, or otherwise obscure? If so, why?
   - Is the purpose justifiable or fair in context?
   - Does the reasoning stay focused on its goal throughout the article?
   - Is the purpose realistic?

2. All news articles focus on a QUESTION or questions that arise from issues or problems considered important.
   - What questions are being addressed in the article?
   - Are there other ways to think about each question being addressed?
   - Can you divide the primary question into sub-questions?
   - Is this a question that has one right answer, or can there be more than one reasonable answer? Does the reporter address all reasonable ways of looking at the issue(s)? If not, why not?
   - Does this question require judgment on the part of the reader, or do the facts alone settle the question?

3. All news articles are based on ASSUMPTIONS.
   - What assumptions is the reporter making—in other words, what is being taken for granted in the article that the reader is not to question? Are these assumptions justified?
   - If the reporter were to begin with a different set of assumptions, how might the article be approached differently?
   - How do your assumptions shape your reading of the article?
   - Which of your assumptions might reasonably be questioned?

4. All news reporting is done from some POINT OF VIEW.
   - What is the point from which the reporter is viewing the issues in the article? What insights is this viewpoint based on? What are its weaknesses?
   - What other points of view should be considered in reasoning through the problem being approached in the article? What are the strengths and weaknesses of these viewpoints? Are you fairmindedly considering the insights behind these viewpoints?

5. All news reporting is based on DATA, INFORMATION, and EVIDENCE.

   - To what extent is the reporter's reasoning supported by relevant and significant data?
   - Do the data suggest explanations that differ from those given by the reporter?
   - How clear, accurate, and relevant are the data to the question at issue?
   - Has the reporter included data sufficient for you to reach a valid conclusion?

6. All news reporting is expressed through, and shaped by, CONCEPTS and THEORIES.

   - What key concepts and theories are guiding the reasoning in the article?
   - What alternative explanations might be possible, given these concepts and theories?
   - Is the reporter clear as to the key concepts and theories being used in the article?
   - Does the reporter distort ideas to fit his or her agenda? If so, why?

7. All news articles contains INFERENCES or INTERPRETATIONS by which we are to draw CONCLUSIONS and give meaning to data.

   - To what extent do the data support the conclusions being advanced by the reporter?
   - Are the inferences in the article consistent with each other?
   - Are there reasonable inferences that should be considered, aside from those being presented by the reporter?

8. All news reporting leads somewhere, that is, has IMPLICATIONS and CONSEQUENCES.

   - What implications and consequences follow from the reasoning embedded in the news article?
   - If we accept the line of reasoning being presented in the article, what implications or consequences are likely? What other implications or consequences are possible or probable?
   - If we ignore the line of reasoning being presented in the article, what implications or consequences are likely? What other implications or consequences are possible or probable?

Evaluate Reasoning Through Critical Thinking Standards

Reasonable people judge reasoning by intellectual standards. When you internalize these standards and explicitly use them in your thinking, your thinking becomes more clear, more accurate, more precise, more relevant, deeper, broader, and more fair. You should note that we focus here on a selection of standards. Among others are credibility, justifiability, reliability, and practicality. Some questions that employ these standards are listed on the following page.

Clarity:
understandable, the meaning can be grasped

Accuracy:
free from errors or distortions, true

Precision:
exact to the necessary level of detail

Relevance:
relating to the matter at hand

Depth:
containing complexities and multiple interrelationships

Breadth:
encompassing multiple viewpoints

Logic:
the parts make sense together, no contradictions

Significance:
focusing on the important, not trivial

Fairness:
justifiable, not self-serving or one-sided

Sufficiency:
including all that is important and relevant to settling a question

Critical Thinking Standards for Assessing News Articles, Editorials, and Stories

Clarity
Is the article, editorial, or story clear?
Are any parts of the article vague?
Are the main points supported by examples?

Accuracy
How can I check the information in this news story or editorial?
How can I find out if this information is true?
Are any facts being ignored or distorted?

Precision
Does the author need to include more details or be more exact?
Are any important details being left out or ignored?

Relevance
Does the author include all the important relevant information?
Is any relevant information being left out? If so, why?

Depth
What are the complexities in the issue?
Are these complexities adequately addressed by the author?
Are any difficulties in the issue being ignored or glossed over?

Breadth
Do I need to look at this issue from another perspective?
Do I need to consider other news sources to get a broader view?

Logic
Does all this make sense together?
Do the author's conclusions follow from the evidence?
Is there a more logical way to interpret the information?

Significance
Is this an important problem to consider?
What significant problems are being ignored in this news story?
Which of the facts in the story are most important?

Fairness
Do I have any vested interest in this issue that may cloud my judgment?
Does this news outlet have a vested interest in covering, or not covering, an important issue?
Does the author represent relevant viewpoints in good faith?
Has the author fully and fairly considered all the important information relevant to the issue?

Sufficiency
Does the author provide sufficient information to address the issue?
Does the author unfairly leave out information he or she would rather not consider or would rather the reader not see? If so, why?

CHARACTERISTICS OF THE DISCIPLINED MIND THAT HELP US DETECT BIAS

Critical consumers of the news cultivate intellectual abilities, as well as intellectual virtues or character traits. These attributes are essential to seeing through propaganda. They determine with what insight and integrity you generally think. Here we briefly describe primary intellectual virtues and suggest questions that foster their development. Only to the extent that you routinely ask these questions of yourself will you develop these virtues.

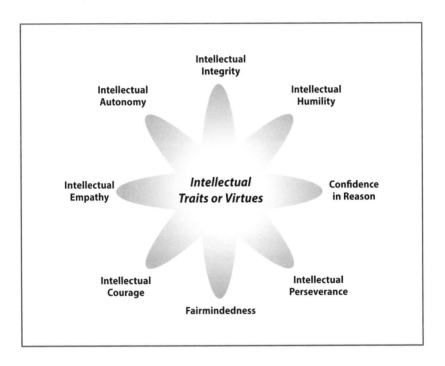

Intellectual
Integrity

Intellectual
Autonomy

Intellectual
Humility

Intellectual
Empathy

*Intellectual
Traits or Virtues*

Confidence
in Reason

Intellectual
Courage

Intellectual
Perseverance

Fairmindedness

Intellectual humility is knowledge of ignorance, that is, sensitivity to what you know and what you do not know. It means being aware of your biases, prejudices, self-deceptive tendencies, and the limitations of your viewpoint. Questions that foster intellectual humility include:

- What do I really know (about myself, about the situation, about another person, about my nation, about what is going on in the world, and about the issues in this news article)?

Are any facts being ignored or distorted in this news story?

- To what extent do my prejudices or biases influence my thinking about this news piece?
- To what extent have I been indoctrinated into beliefs that may be false?
- How do the beliefs I have uncritically accepted keep me from seeing this news article in an unbiased way?

Intellectual courage is the disposition to question beliefs you feel strongly about, some of which you may have held over a lifetime. It includes questioning the beliefs of your culture and the groups to which you belong, and a willingness to express your views even when they are unpopular. Questions that foster intellectual courage include:

- To what extent have I analyzed my beliefs?
- To what extent have I questioned the beliefs that guide my judgment about the news, many of which I learned in childhood?
- To what extent have I demonstrated a willingness to give up my beliefs when sufficient evidence is presented against them?
- To what extent am I willing to stand up against the majority (even though people might ridicule me)?
- Do I have the courage to seek alternative news sources to check mainstream news outlets for accuracy and reasonability?

Intellectual empathy is awareness of the need to actively entertain views that differ from our own, especially those we strongly disagree with. It is to accurately reconstruct the viewpoints and reasoning of our opponents and to reason from premises, assumptions, and ideas other than our own. Questions that foster intellectual empathy include:

- To what extent do I accurately represent viewpoints I disagree with?
- Could I summarize the views of my opponents to their satisfaction? Can I see insights in the views of others and prejudices in my own?
- Do I sympathize with the feelings of others in light of their thinking differently from me?
- To what extent can I reason within alternative news sources to balance my view?

Intellectual integrity consists in holding yourself to the same standards you expect others to honor (no double standards). Questions that foster intellectual integrity include:

- Do I behave in accordance with what I say I believe, or do I tend to say one thing and do another?
- To what extent do I expect the same of myself as I expect of others?

- To what extent do I expect the same high standards of "my group" as I expect of other groups?
- To what extent are there contradictions or inconsistencies in my life?
- To what extent do I strive to recognize and eliminate self-deception in all parts of my life, including the way I perceive the news?
- To what extent do I seek news sources that hold all parties to the same high standards?

Intellectual perseverance is the disposition to work your way through intellectual complexities, despite frustrations inherent in the process. Questions that foster intellectual perseverance include:

- Am I willing to work my way through complexities in an issue, or do I tend to give up when I experience difficulty?
- Can I think of a difficult intellectual problem in which I have demonstrated patience and determination in working through the difficulties?
- Do I have strategies for dealing with complex problems I run across in the news?
- Do I expect learning from "the news" to be easy, or do I recognize the importance of working through complexities to find out what is really going on in the world?

Confidence in reason is based on the belief that one's own higher interests and those of humankind at large are best served by giving free play to reason. It means using standards of reasonability as the fundamental criteria by which to accept or reject any belief or position. Questions that foster confidence in reason include:

Does the reporter include all the important relevant information?

- Am I willing to change my position when the evidence leads to a more reasonable one?
- Do I adhere to principles of sound reasoning when persuading others of my position, or do I distort matters to support my position?
- Do I deem it more important to "win" an argument, or, instead, to see the issue from the most reasonable perspective?
- Do I encourage others to come to their own conclusions, or do I try to force my views on them?
- Am I open to facts and evidence as revealed in the news media, or, alternatively, do I seek other information that may or may not be true in order to maintain my position?

Intellectual autonomy is thinking for oneself while adhering to standards of rationality. It means thinking through issues using one's own thinking rather than uncritically accepting the viewpoints of others. Questions that foster intellectual autonomy include:

- To what extent do I conform to the views of others uncritically?
- To what extent do I confine my news exposure habits to well-written mainstream or alternative sources, or, on the other hand, to sources that routinely distort or misrepresent the news in ways that fit my perspective?
- To what extent do I uncritically accept what I am told by my government, the media, or my peers?
- Do I think through the news on my own, using my best reasoning, or am I easily bamboozled by the news media and politicians?
- Having thought through an issue from a rational perspective, am I willing to stand alone despite the irrational criticisms of others?

RATIONAL CAPACITIES OR IRRATIONAL TENDENCIES CAN CONTROL THE MIND

To take command of the way we interpret and understand the news, we must see that the way we think and feel about the news is guided and directed either by our native irrationality or, conversely, our rational capacities.

Irrational tendencies function automatically and largely unconsciously. Rational tendencies, on the other hand, tend to arise from active self-development and are largely conscious. Irrationality can be principally viewed in terms of two broad and overlapping categories: egocentric and sociocentric thought.

Egocentric thought, as we refer to it in our work, is focused on the pursuit of one's own desires and needs without regard to the rights and needs of others. Sociocentric thought is focused on the pursuit of group goals without regard to the rights and needs of those outside the group. In this section we briefly detail and unpack the concepts of egocentric and sociocentric thought, in juxtaposition with rationality or reasonability.[1]

Egocentrism

Egocentrism exists in two forms: skilled and unskilled. Both pursue selfish ends. Highly skilled egocentric persons use their intelligence to effectively rationalize gaining their selfish ends at the expense of others. They skillfully distort information to serve their interests. They are often articulate in arguing for their ends (which they typically cover with altruistic language). They hide their prejudices well.

---

1   For more on the dual problem of egocentric and sociocentric thought in human life, see *The Thinker's Guide to the Human Mind* by Linda Elder and Richard Paul (Lanham, MD: Rowman & Littlefield, reprint edition, 2015).

Naïve others often fail to see the selfish core of egocentric people (masked, as it is, in an ethical or seemingly considerate façade). Successful egocentric people often succeed in moving up the social ladder, and in gaining prestigious jobs and honored positions. Skilled egocentric persons may favor either domination or submission in getting their way, but often combine both in effective ways. For example, they may successfully dominate persons "below" them while being subtly servile to those "above" them. They know how to tell people what they want to hear. They are consummate manipulators and often hold positions of power. Skilled egocentric news reporters and agencies effectively manipulate naïve consumers of the news.

Unskilled egocentric persons are unsuccessful in pursuing their selfish ends, because many people see through them and do not trust them. Their prejudices and narrowness are more obvious and less schooled. They often have blatantly dysfunctional relationships with others. They are often trapped in negative emotions they do not understand. Unskilled egocentric persons may

> Is the purpose of the news article clear, or is the purpose muddled, vague, or otherwise obscure? If so, why?

prefer either domination or submission as a means of getting what they want, but whichever they use, they are usually unsuccessful. Sometimes they are overtly cruel or play the victim in openly self-pitying ways.

Sociocentrism

As humans, we are all born centered in ourselves. As part of our native egocentrism, we feel directly and unavoidably our own pain and frustration, our own joy and pleasure. We largely see the world from a narrow, self-serving perspective.

But we humans are also social animals. We must interact with others to survive as beings in the world. In interacting with others in groups, we form complex belief systems. These belief systems often reflect a variety of forms of intellectual blindness as well as intellectual insights. In living a human life, we develop worldviews that are a mixture of self-serving, group-serving, and rational thought.

Our social groups not only provide us with ways and means of surviving; they also impose on us relatively narrow ways of looking at the world, and they powerfully influence our thoughts and actions. Our intrinsic narrowness of perspective, focused on our own needs and wants, merges with our group views as we are increasingly socialized and conditioned, over time, to see the world not only from our own point of view, but from the perspectives of our groups: family, gender, peers, colleagues, ethnic group, nationality, religion, profession, and so forth.

Sociocentric thought is the native human tendency to see the world from narrow and biased group-centered perspectives, to operate within the world through group rules in pursuit of group interests. It is intimately connected with the perceived innate human need to be accepted and esteemed by others.

As we will elaborate later, sociocentrism is at the heart of most of the bias and propaganda found in the media and throughout politics. Since humans largely see the world from their groups' perspectives and therefore through the lenses of their groups' prejudices and arbitrary social customs, they seek "news" (however biased) that validates their groups' preconceptions.

Rationality

Rationality is properly thought of as a way of thinking and acting in which intelligence and sound reasoning are used to serve justice, in which reasoners adhere to the same standards by which they judge their enemies, in which they do not need to rationalize or project a false façade to impress others. Successful powerful people are often intelligent, unreasonable, and unscrupulous—all in one. They often cannot openly admit the games they play to obtain social and economic success; they frequently suppress evidence that puts them in a bad light.

Do I need to look at this issue from another perspective? Do I need to consider other news sources to get a broader view?

Reasonable people, on the other hand, respect the rights and needs of others. They are flexible, open-minded, and just. They embody intellectual integrity as well as intellectual humility and intellectual perseverance. They have confidence in reason and therefore follow the evidence wherever it may lead them. They are able to enter empathically into the viewpoints of others. They do not misuse language in order to manipulate people and hide unsavory motives. They say what they mean and mean what they say.

Rationality is sometimes wrongly thought of as encompassing both those who intelligently and successfully pursue selfish ends and those who intelligently and successfully pursue unselfish ends. We disagree. Instead, we believe that those who intelligently pursue selfish ends are those described as skilled egocentric persons. In other words, we do not think that those who sophistically manipulate people to act against their interests, and consequently lack integrity, are properly called "reasonable" persons. Consummate manipulators, however skilled and successful, are not reasonable persons (since they would be the first to object to being treated as they routinely treat others).

News agencies and reporters who embrace ethical rationality as a way of life do not seek to distort the news or in any way mislead people. Instead, they present the most important news as they understand it, offer all reasonable sides of the issues embedded in it, and welcome discussion and debate among their readers.

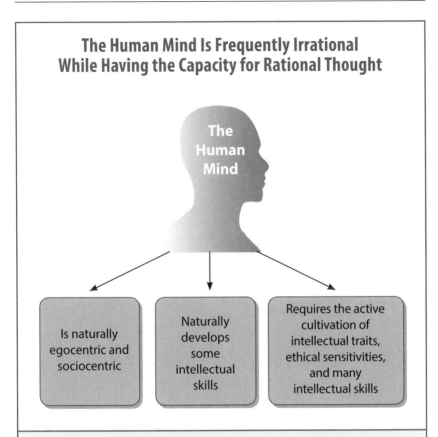

The Human Mind Is Frequently Irrational While Having the Capacity for Rational Thought

The Human Mind

Is naturally egocentric and sociocentric

Naturally develops some intellectual skills

Requires the active cultivation of intellectual traits, ethical sensitivities, and many intellectual skills

Essential Idea: All humans are innately egocentric and sociocentric. Humans also have (largely undeveloped) rational capacities. Humans begin life as primarily egocentric creatures. Over time, infantile egocentric self-centered thinking merges with sociocentric group-centered thinking. All humans regularly engage in both forms of irrational thought. The extent to which any of us is egocentric or sociocentric is a matter of degree and can change significantly in various situations or contexts. While egocentric and sociocentric propensities are naturally occurring phenomena, rational capacities must be largely developed. It is through the development of rational capacities that we combat irrational tendencies and cultivate critical societies.

Distinguishing Rational from Egocentric and Sociocentric Motives

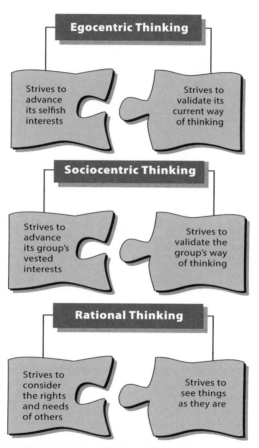

Egocentric Thinking

Strives to advance its selfish interests

Strives to validate its current way of thinking

Sociocentric Thinking

Strives to advance its group's vested interests

Strives to validate the group's way of thinking

Rational Thinking

Strives to consider the rights and needs of others

Strives to see things as they are

Essential Idea: Though egocentric, sociocentric, and rational thought may be complex, we can capture their basic motives.

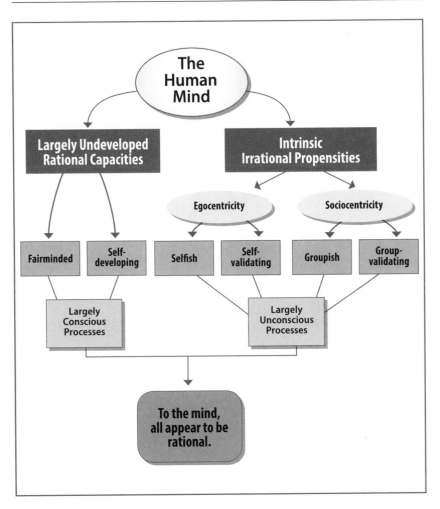

Humans Often Distort Reality Through Irrational Lenses

When engaging in irrational pursuits, the mind must deceive itself; it relies on pathologies of thought to do it. The pathologies of thought can be pictured as a set of filters or lenses that:

- cause or "enable" us to see the world according to our perceived interests, without regard to others,
- distort reality so we can get what we want,
- lead us to ignore relevant information to paint a favored picture of the world, based on our vested interests.

These pathologies allow us to deceive ourselves into believing what we want to believe (in order to get what we want or maintain our viewpoint). Pathologies of thought, hence, serve their master—self-deception. They are mainfest in both egocentric and sociocentric thought.

(To deepen your understanding of irrationality, work through *Think for Yourself 3: Identifying Irrational Lenses and Their Consequences* in Appendix A.)

The Problem of Egocentric Thinking

Egocentric thinking comes from the unfortunate fact that humans do not naturally consider the rights and needs of others, nor do we naturally appreciate the point of view of others or the limitations in our own point of view. We become explicitly aware of our egocentric thinking only if trained to do so. We do not naturally recognize our egocentric assumptions, the egocentric way we use information, the egocentric way we interpret data, the source of our egocentric concepts and ideas, the implications of our egocentric thought. We do not naturally recognize our self-serving perspective.

As humans we live with the unrealistic but confident sense that we have fundamentally figured out the way things actually are, and that we have done this objectively. We naturally believe in our intuitive perceptions—however inaccurate. Instead of using intellectual standards in thinking, we often use self-centered psychological standards to determine what to believe and what to reject. Here are the most commonly used psychological standards in human thinking:

"IT'S TRUE BECAUSE I BELIEVE IT." *Innate egocentrism:* I assume that what I believe is true even though I have never questioned the basis for many of my beliefs.

"IT'S TRUE BECAUSE I WANT TO BELIEVE IT." *Innate wish fulfillment:* I believe in, for example, accounts of behavior that put me (or the groups to which I belong) in a positive rather than a negative light even though I have not seriously considered the evidence for the more negative account. I believe what "feels good," what supports my other beliefs, what does not require me to change my thinking in any significant way, what does not require me to admit I have been wrong.

"IT'S TRUE BECAUSE I HAVE ALWAYS BELIEVED IT." *Innate self-validation:* I have a strong desire to maintain beliefs that I have long held, even though I have not seriously considered the extent to which those beliefs are justified, given the evidence.

"IT'S TRUE BECAUSE IT IS IN MY SELFISH INTEREST TO BELIEVE IT." *Innate selfishness:* I hold fast to beliefs that justify my getting more power, money, or personal advantage even though these beliefs are not grounded in sound reasoning or evidence.

Since humans are naturally prone to assess thinking in keeping with the above criteria, it is not surprising that we, as a species, have not developed a significant interest in establishing and advancing legitimate intellectual standards. It is not surprising that we are easily persuaded by news that fits our egocentric agendas.

The Problem of Sociocentric Thinking

Consider four distinct forms of sociocentric thought. These forms function and are manifest in complex relationships with one another; all are destructive.[1] They can be summarized as follows:

1. *Groupishness*[2] *(or group selfishness)*—the tendency on the part of groups to seek the most for the in-group without regard to the rights and needs of others, in order to advance the group's biased interests. Groupishness is almost certainly the primary tendency in sociocentric thinking, the foundational driving force behind it (probably connected to survival in our dim dark past). Everyone in the group is privileged; everyone outside the group is denied group privileges and/or seen as a potential threat.

2. *Group validation*—the tendency on the part of groups to believe their way to be the right way and their views to be the correct views; the tendency to reinforce one another in these beliefs; the inclination to validate the group's views, however dysfunctional or illogical. These may be long-held or newly established views, but in either case, they are perceived by the group to be true and in many cases to advance its interests. This tendency informs the worldview from which everyone outside the group is seen and understood and by which everything that happens outside the group is judged. It leads to the problem of *in-group* thinking and behavior—everyone inside the group thinking within a collective logic; everyone outside the group being judged according to the standards and beliefs of the in-group.

---

1   The term sociocentric thought is being reserved for those group beliefs that cause harm or are likely to cause harm. Group thought that is reasonable, useful, or helpful would not fall into this category. In our view, it is important to see sociocentric thought as destructive because otherwise the mind will find a variety of ways to rationalize it. By recognizing it as irrational, we are better able to identify it in our thinking and take command of it.

2   By groupishness we mean group selfishness. This term refers to group pursuit of its interests without sufficient regard for the rights and needs of those outside the group; its counterpart is selfishness, which refers to individual pursuit of one's interests without sufficient regard for the rights and needs of others. We might use the term "group selfishness" for our intended meaning here; but it seems rather to be an oxymoron. How can a group be selfish, given the root word "self," which refers to the individual? The term "groupish" seems a better fit for the purpose. Note that this use of the term "groupish" differs from the way in which evolutionary biologists use the same term. Their use generally refers to the fact that members of a group are aware of their group membership and are aware that there are others (like them) in the group.

3. *Group control*—the tendency on the part of groups to ensure that group members behave in accordance with group expectations. This logic guides the intricate inner workings of the group, largely through enforcement, ostracism, and punishment in connection with group customs, conventions, rules, taboos, mores, and laws. Group control can also take the form of "recruitment" through propaganda and other forms of manipulation. It is often sophisticated and camouflaged.

4. *Group conformity*—a byproduct of the fact that to survive, people must figure out how to fit themselves into the groups they are thrust into or voluntarily choose to join. They must conform to the rules and laws set down by those in control. Dissenters are punished in numerous ways. Group control and group conformity are two sides of the same coin—each presupposes the other.

These four sociocentric tendencies interrelate and overlap in any number of ways and thus should be understood as four parts of an interconnected puzzle.

Sociocentric tendencies largely lie at the unconscious level. It isn't that people are aware of these tendencies and consciously choose to go along with them. Rather, these dispositions are, at least to some extent, hidden by self-deception, rationalization, and other native mechanisms of the mind that keep us from seeing and facing the truth in our thoughts and actions. The mind tells itself one thing on the surface (e.g., we are being fair to all involved) when in fact it is acting upon a different thought entirely (e.g., we are mainly concerned with our own interests). In most instances, the mind can find ways to justify itself—even when engaging in highly unethical acts.[3]

---

3   It should be pointed out that there are many circumstances where rational behavior might be confused with sociocentric behavior. For instance, group members may well validate among themselves views that are reasonable. And groups should expect group members to behave in ethical ways. There may also be many other conditions under which it would make sense for an individual to conform to group expectations (e.g. to keep from being tortured or to contribute to the well being of the planet).

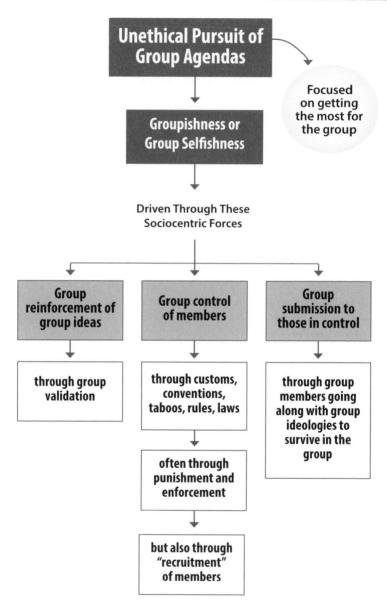

Groupishness, to be effectively "achieved," requires group reinforcement, group control, and group submission; this diagram begins to illuminate the complex relationships between and among the four primary forms of sociocentric thought.

With these foundations in place, as we move forward in the book, you will see how the basic concepts and principles in critical thinking are essential to understanding the logic of the news and protecting yourself against bias and propaganda of all types.

CHAPTER 3

OBJECTIVITY, BIASES, AND UNDERLYING AGENDAS

Nothing could be more irrational than to give the people power and to withhold from them information, without which power is abused. A people who mean to be their own governors must arm themselves with the power which knowledge gives. A popular government without popular information or the means of acquiring it is but a prologue to a farce or a tragedy, or perhaps both.

—JAMES MADISON

DEMOCRACY AND THE NEWS MEDIA

Democracy can be an effective form of government only to the extent that the public (that rules the government in theory) is well-informed about national and international events and can think independently and critically about those events. If the vast majority of citizens do not recognize bias in their nation's news; if they cannot detect ideology, slant, and spin; if they cannot recognize propaganda when exposed to it, they cannot reasonably determine what media messages have to be supplemented, counterbalanced, or thrown out entirely.

On the one hand, worldwide news sources are increasingly sophisticated in media logic (the art of "persuading" and manipulating large masses of people). This enables news outlets to create an aura of objectivity and "truthfulness" in the news stories they construct. On the other hand, only a small minority of people are skilled in recognizing bias and propaganda in the news disseminated in their country. Only a few are able to detect one-sided portrayals of events or seek out alternative sources of information and opinion to compare to those of their mainstream news media. At present, the overwhelming majority of people in the world, untrained in critical thinking, are at the mercy of the news media in their own country. Their view of the world, including which countries and groups they identify as friends and which as enemies, is determined largely by those media (and the traditional beliefs and conventions of their society).

This slanted information is not a "plot" or a "conspiracy." It is simply a matter of educational background and economic reality. Journalists and news editors are themselves members of a culture (German, French, Mexican, Chinese, Korean, Japanese, Indonesian, Russian, Algerian, Nigerian, North American, and so on). They share a view of the world with their target audiences. They share a nationalized sense of history and allegiance, often a religion, and a general belief system. An Arab editor sees the world through different lenses than does an Israeli editor. A Pakistani editor sees the world differently from an Indian one. A Chinese editor sees the world differently from an American one. In any country, news outlets also advance differing political and ideological perspectives. The same is true of news reporters.

What is more, news people work under severe time restrictions (in constructing their stories) and limitations of space (in laying out or presenting their stories). It is hardly surprising that profound differences are reflected in news coverage from nation to nation, culture to culture, and group to group.

In any case, only those who understand the conditions under which world media operate have a chance of controlling the influence of the news media upon them. It is in all of our interests to critically assess, rather than mindlessly accept, news media pronouncements. Our hope is that we can aid you in becoming more independent, insightful, and critical in responding to the content of news media messages and stories. (To deepen your understanding of differing worldviews, and how these worldviews are treated by the news media, work through *Think for Yourself 4: Contrasting Worldviews* in Appendix A.)

MYTHS THAT OBSCURE THE LOGIC OF THE NEWS MEDIA

The media foster a set of myths regarding how they function. Believing these myths impedes your ability to view the news from a critical perspective. These myths include:

- That most news stories are produced through independent investigative journalism.
- That news writers simply report facts in their stories and do not offer their conclusions or interpretations about them.
- That fact and opinion are clearly separated in constructing the news.
- That there is an objective reality (the actual "news") that is simply "reported" or described by news media (with "our" news media writers reporting on this objectively, and the media of foreign enemies or political opponents systematically slanting and distorting it).
- That what is unusual (novel, odd, bizarre) is news; what is usual is not.

BIAS AND OBJECTIVITY IN THE NEWS MEDIA

The logic of constructing news stories is parallel to the logic of writing history. In both cases, for events covered, there is both a massive background of facts and a highly restricted amount of space, time, and other resources to devote to those facts. The result in both cases is the same: 99.99999% of the "facts" are never mentioned at all.

The % recorded as "news"

If objectivity or fairness in the construction of news stories is thought of as equivalent to presenting all the facts and only the facts ("all the news that's fit to print"), objectivity and fairness is an illusion. No human knows more than a small percentage of the facts, and it is not possible to present all the facts even if one could know them. It isn't even possible to present all the important facts, for many criteria compete for determining what is "important." We must therefore always ask,

- What has been left out of this article?
- How might I think differently if different facts had been highlighted here?
- What if this article had been written by those who hold a point of view opposite to the one embedded in the story as told?

For example, people commonly consider facts to be important to the extent that they have significant implications for them personally: Is any given event going to affect what they want? How much is it going to cost them? How is it going to influence their income, their living conditions, their leisure, and their convenience?

In contrast, how some given event is going to affect others, especially others far away and out of sight, is more easily ignored or played down. There is therefore a large divergence among the news media of the world as to what is presented as "significant" in the world.

> What has been left out of this article?

The media focus on what their readers personally care about. Thus, even if their readers hold absurd or unreasonable beliefs (such as harboring irrational hatred toward some groups), the media pandering to these news consumers nevertheless will treat that hatred as rational. Hence, when slavery was commonly accepted in the United States, the news media presented slavery as "natural." When the country became divided on the issue, the news media followed suit, with each newspaper presenting as right what its readers believed to be right. (To deepen your understanding of the points in this section, work through *Think for Yourself 5: Identifying the Promotion of Irrational Viewpoints Disguised as Rational Ones* in Appendix A.)

Consider how news media treat what is "shocking," "exciting," "disgusting," or "delightful" to a social group. For example, a woman sun-bathing on a beach with bare breasts is commonplace on the French Riviera and therefore is not condemned, nor is her behavior treated as "news"; but the same woman would be arrested and punished for sun-bathing in a similar way at a beach in Lebanon. Her behavior would likely therefore be condemned and treated as "news" by her local news media.

Or, again, during the Olympics, each country's news media focus their attention on those events in which their nation's athletes are expected to do well. When one of their athletes wins a gold medal in an event, this event is presented to the home audience as if it were much more important than the events in which they won no medals. National audiences often are "thrilled" by "their victories" and uninterested in the victories of others.

How might I think differently if different facts had been highlighted in this news story?

These people are usually completely unaware of the fact that if they lived in other countries, they would blindly cheer for the teams in those nations, rather than for the teams they currently associate themselves with.

Human "objectivity" is an ideal no one perfectly achieves. Striving for it requires a great deal of intellectual humility (knowledge of our extensive ignorance) and begins by freely admitting one's own point of view, as well as the need to consider competing sources of information and opinion when making important judgments.

The key point is this: there are typically multiple points of view from which any set of events can be viewed and interpreted. Openness to a range of insights from multiple points of view and willingness to question one's own point of view are crucial to "objectivity." This can be suggested in a diagram that illustrates how multiple viewpoints often stand in relation to the same set of events (see diagram, page 47). Objectivity is achieved to the extent that one has studied a wide range of perspectives relevant to an issue, obtained insights from all of them, seen weaknesses and partiality in each, and integrated what one has learned into a more comprehensive, many-sided whole. Each should serve to "correct" exaggerations or distortions in the others, and to add facts not highlighted in the others.

Six Points of View Focused on the Same Set of Events

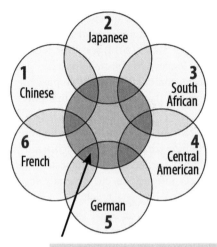

2 Japanese

1 Chinese

3 South African

6 French

4 Central American

German 5

Note:

- Only some of the facts are highlighted in any point of view
- All points of view ignore or play down some facts
- No single point of view provides total understanding
- Understanding multiple viewpoints increases insight

The total set of facts relevant to understanding a given set of events

In conceptualizing both history and the news, we gain "objectivity" to the extent that we can put stories and narratives into a rich historical context and comment on them from multiple points of view. For example, to understand the war between Britain and its colonies in North America (1776–1783), one must look at the events from at least three points of view: that of the British government, that of the Colonial leaders, and that of the indigenous peoples.

To achieve objectivity, we need to:

1. Identify the point of view from which a given news story or historical account is constructed,
2. Identify the audience it is targeting (or pandering to),
3. Recognize what points of view it is negating or ignoring, and
4. Distinguish the raw facts behind the story from the interpretation and spin being put on those facts.

When we do this, we are not as easily manipulated.

When we think critically about the news, we are able to exercise independence of judgment. We achieve a greater sense of what elements of the story or account are most or least credible. We know how to discover multiple sources of information, and we can question whether and to what degree sources are credible. (To deepen your understanding of the points in this section, work through *Think for Yourself 6: Identifying the Interests of Readers* in Appendix A.)

HOW THE NEWS MEDIA VIEW OBJECTIVITY TODAY

Due to current perspectives on objectivity, there now seems to be debate among journalists as to whether and to what extent objectivity can be achieved, or even whether it should be attempted in news reporting. Atkins (2016) says: "the code of the Society of Professional Journalism (SPJ) no longer lists objectivity as a core goal. According to Brent Cunningham of Columbia Journalism Review, SPJ dropped the term 'objectivity' from the code due to the dilemma that the term tends to mean different things to different people" (p. 11).

But there are agreed-upon definitions and conceptions of objectivity, and these we should pay attention to. If we take our definition from the *Oxford English Dictionary* (2019 online, Oxford University Press), we find the term "objectivity" to refer to "the ability to consider or represent facts, information, etc. without being influenced by personal feelings or opinions; impartiality; detachment."

If we take objectivity to mean "never taking a stand on an issue," we stretch the use too far, since it is possible to take a stand on an issue and yet address it without prejudice or bias. And if by objectivity we are to view all stories as equally important, again, we misuse the term. Some issues are by their very nature pressing, given current events and precisely where one is situated at a particular time in history. For instance, the problem of the earth's warming, which now threatens many species worldwide, as well as the very health of the earth itself, should be a primary source of news stories, now and until the problems at the heart of human-induced climate change are addressed (which may never be). To say that the media is biased when it focuses on the problem of climate change and the science behind it is to misuse the term bias—in order to serve another interest usually related to money and power on the opposing side. In other words, it is easy for someone to claim media bias and lack of objectivity when a covered story does not agree with one's own biased views. This is a form of projection prevalent in human cultures.

As we have pointed out, journalists are naturally biased according to not only their worldviews and perspectives, but also those of the news outlets that employ them. In the final analysis, the extent to which any reporter is biased, and in precisely what ways, will be a matter of degree and depend on circumstances.

FORMS OF OBJECTIVITY

"Objectivity" on the part of the news consumer, and news outlet or reporter, may appear in at least three ways. Two are genuine. One is a fake or a counterfeit of objectivity.

The Objectivity of Intellectual Humility

The first form of objectivity is based on the possibility of developing intellectual humility or knowledge of our ignorance. Thus, a critical consumer of the news knows the difference between hearing a story and verifying the truth of that story.

A critical consumer of the news knows that what is presented as fact in the news may not be fact. It may be propaganda, misinformation, distortion, or half-truth. Knowing this, critical consumers of the news "bracket" what they hear, read, and see in the news. Recognizing that they don't themselves know the facts, they suspend belief. They take in information in a tentative fashion ("This may or may not be true!"). For example, "objective" jurors will not come to a conclusion of guilt or innocence after hearing only one side's case. News outlets and reporters who value intellectual humility and attempt to embody it are aware when they lack information to take a position on an issue.

Unfortunately, intellectual humility is a rare quality in human life. The majority of people in the world have been exposed to a limited range of views and have been most influenced by the viewpoints dominant in their own country, culture, and social set. Yet, they take themselves to be in possession

> What if this article had been written by those who hold a point of view opposite to the one embedded in the story as told? How would it be written differently?

of "the TRUTH." This confidence is in fact proof of their lack of objectivity and their embodiment of intellectual arrogance. They neither know what intellectual humility is, nor take steps to achieve it.

The Objectivity of Fairminded, Multidimensional Thinking

A second form of objectivity goes beyond the first. It is based on intellectual humility and also on having done substantial intellectual work in reasoning within multiple conflicting points of view in addressing questions, problems, and issues of significance. It entails positive insight into the complications and many-sidedness of most important world issues and large-scale conflicts. Those who have achieved this state can insightfully role-play multiple perspectives on a multitude of issues. They can identify and weigh relative strengths and weaknesses within those perspectives. They are comfortable playing the role of dissenter, though they don't dissent for the sake of argument or to be disagreeable. They reject party lines, sociocentric mind-sets, and intellectual conformity. They are intellectually independent, intellectually perseverant, and persons of intellectual integrity.

News consumers who embody this characteristic open-mindedly consider all important aspects of a news story and seek to understand the complexities within these aspects before coming to firm conclusions about the story. They do not think in sound bites and are properly annoyed by the almost constant oversimplification found in the news. Often, critical reasoners realize they cannot accept an argument or position taken in a news story or editorial because they do not themselves understand the complexities and difficulties within the questions at issue embedded in the news story or editorial. This happens when news reporters fail to detail the important information relevant to reasoning through a complex issue or set of issues.

News writers and outlets who embody fairminded, multidimensional thinking attempt at all times to offer the best reasoning for all the significant positions on an issue, and to objectively report the news as they understand it. They do not hide, either from themselves or others, information they would rather not consider. Instead they openly and honestly report the news and let the readers come to their own conclusions. Ideally, reporters would offer the highest-level reasoning from all significant viewpoints and ask readers to decide for themselves what positions seem best to take on the issues. But this is rarely achieved, due, again, to limited space and time, as well as inherent biases on the part of reporters and news outlets, and the very ways in which news is conceptualized (typically brief and superficial). (To deepen your understanding of the points in this section, work through *Think for Yourself 7: Identifying News Outlets That Exemplify Fairminded, Multidimensional Thinking* in Appendix A.)

Are facts and conclusions mixed together in this news story? Which are facts and which are interpretations?

Sophistic Objectivity

The third form of objectivity is "sophistic." This perspective results from studying a range of views with the overriding motivation to defend a predetermined and biased choice. This mindset is common in intellectuals who make their income and achieve their prestige as champions for powerful interests. The temptation to defend a well-established point of view or economic interest is enormous due to the money, position, and prestige typically involved. Lawyers and politicians, as well as public relations professionals, are typically ready to play such a role. Many advocacy journalists and news commentators routinely play such a role. They present positions consistent with a picture of the world shared by their readers or viewers. Reporters and commentators are typically viewed by their audience as "objective" only to the extent that what they present reflects the views of the audience.

THE PERCEPTION OF BIAS IN THE MAINSTREAM

Quite naturally, but uncritically, people think of those who agree with them as objective and those who disagree with them as biased. Thus, if news commentators present mainstream views with a liberal spin, they are viewed as "objective" only by liberals. If mainstream views are given a conservative spin, they are viewed as "objective" only by conservatives. Consequently, the media present liberal or conservative slants on the news in accordance with their audience's views.

PROPAGANDA AND NEWS STORY WRITING

Webster's *New World Dictionary* defines propaganda as "any systematic, widespread dissemination or promotion of particular ideas, doctrines, practices, etc., to further one's own cause or to damage an opposing one." Given this definition, there is no clear-cut dividing line between news writing with a given cultural audience in mind, on the one hand, and constructing propaganda, on the other hand. Both systematically play down or seek to minimize the worth of opposing perspectives or points of view. The logical similarity is striking. Even historical writing can take on the character of propaganda when it is written to "glorify" or "demonize" certain groups of people by suppressing or ignoring information that does not support its preconceptions and favored ideology.

Because the word "propaganda" carries with it a negative connotation (suggesting deception or distortion), few news writers would admit that the word applies to their stories. Yet the fact remains that if one receives most of one's news from a single cultural, national, or political source, the likely impact on the mind will be that of distortion and deception. Most people, as a result, are trapped in one worldview, because they have received a steady diet of stories and accounts articulated from that perspective and have not seriously considered alternatives.

This does not mean, of course, that a given worldview is unvaried. Not everyone who shares a viewpoint agrees on every issue. Of course, not every German agrees with every other German, yet a significant difference exists between those who see the world from a German perspective and those who see it from, say, a Japanese or Mexican perspective. What is more, though virtually every point of view carries some insight, it doesn't follow that there is equal insight in all of them.

It is usually much easier for people to recognize the truth of these tendencies when thinking about news coverage in other nations or cultures—especially when those other nations and cultures differ greatly from their own. Israelis easily recognize bias and propaganda in Arab coverage, though they see little in their own, and vice versa.

When President George W. Bush of the United States gave a speech identifying Iran, Iraq, and North Korea as an "axis of evil," his speech was favorably received by the majority of Americans. It was taken as a follow-up of the president's promise to "rid the world of evil." A wave of patriotic fervor was sweeping the nation. The national news media had engendered a communal sense of anger, angst, and urgency. To the overwhelming majority of Americans, the American government stands for high ideals such as liberty, justice, democracy, free enterprise, and human rights. The president seeming to defend the country against its enemies with the might of its armed forces is an image that inspires patriotic emotions.

The speech, however, was not received in the same way abroad. President Bush was roundly condemned by the news media in Iran, Iraq, and North Korea, and was also viewed as arrogant and out of touch with the complexities of reality by many allies of the United States.

Here are some of the ways the French and German media conceptualized the speech to their national audiences:[1]

- "In France, the afternoon daily Le Monde ran a front-page cartoon of Mr. Bush in battle fatigues and a headline saying, 'Mr. Bush points out his latest enemies.'"
- "A television editorialist on LCI, France's 24-hour news station, said the speech belonged to 'a sheriff convinced of his right to regulate the planet and impose punishment as he sees fit.'"
- "In Germany, an editorial in the daily Sueddeutsche Zeitung offered Chancellor Gerhard Schroder sympathy as he heads for Washington tonight. '"Poor Gerhard Schroder,' the editorial says. 'It can't be easy being the first grumpy European to appear at the throne of the freshly anointed American Caesar.'"

Here is a sense of the news media coverage in Iran and North Korea:

- An Iranian state radio report stated, "Bush intends to divert public opinion from the Middle East issue and to prepare the domestic grounds for continuing his support of Israel in its brutal oppression of the Palestinian nation."
- "North Korea's official media scoffed at Mr. Bush for identifying the nation as among the world's most dangerous. It said his 'loudmouthed threat' was intended to justify an American military presence in South Korea."

Of course, in virtually every case, it is easier to persuade people that "foreign" press coverage is biased than to persuade those same people of bias in their own national press. Every nation's press coverage of the "news" appears to the mass public of that culture as expressing self-evident truth—because the news is routinely presented within the worldview of the mass public that "consumes" that news. When exceptions to this pattern exist, it is because a given news outlet takes a significantly

---

1   All of the quotes in this section were taken from the *New York Times*, January 31, 2002, p. A12.

different political, economic, or social position than that of the news consumer; noticing one's own tendencies in this regard is a prerequisite for questioning and accurately assessing news sources within one's national as well as the foreign press.

When trapped in a culture-bound view of the world, one thinks within a web of self-serving assumptions, thinking that it is others—that is, our national or cultural enemies and opponents—who use propaganda and manipulation while we, being honest and just, always give the other side its due. "Others" use propaganda and manipulation. "We" freely express the truth. This mind-set is not the product of a conspiracy or intrigue; it is the natural and predictable outcome of national news media attempting to make a profit by presenting events in the world to a home audience. (To deepen your understanding of propaganda in the news, work through *Think for Yourself 8: Exploring Propaganda in the News* in Appendix A.)

PROTECTING THE HOME AUDIENCE FROM GUILT FEELINGS

The events for which news coverage is most taboo in mainstream media news are deeds that indict the home culture or society of ethical wrongdoing. Consider, for example, the extent of civilian suffering following the dropping of atomic bombs on the cities of Hiroshima and Nagasaki by the U.S. military. Though some debate has taken place in the U.S. media on these acts, to our knowledge, the American mainstream media have presented little documentation of the enormous suffering caused by those events.

One might compare, for example, documentation of the suffering of civilians in German extermination camps (which has been and continues to be extensive) with that of the Japanese populations of Hiroshima and Nagasaki through exposure to massive radiation. Scanning the almost 80 years of press coverage since the

> What is the point of view from which the reporter is viewing the issues in the article? What insights is this viewpoint based on? What are its weaknesses?

event, we found very few articles focused on the United States dropping bombs on Japan's civilians. One editorial, in the *Santa Rosa Press Democrat* (*Hiroshima Victims Recall Horror*, March 21, 2002) documented in detail the suffering of the civilian population. The article was a guest editorial by David R. Ford, who worked in 1965 for a CBS television affiliate in Honolulu and is presently living in the Santa Rosa, California area. Here are excerpts (without the horrific details) from his editorial (p. 17):

"In 1965 . . . I spent a vacation in Hiroshima, Japan. My purpose: To interview the sick and dying 20 years after the atomic bomb was exploded over that city on Aug. 6, 1944 . . . I began the visit in the women's ward."

What follows in the article are detailed images of suffering that American readers would find extremely painful to imagine their government inflicting. The American reporter said to a Japanese victim, "'But we dropped millions of pamphlets warning citizens to evacuate the cities.' He looked into my eyes. 'No paper was ever dropped. No warning was ever given.'"

We cannot, of course, attest to the truth or falsity of the allegation of U.S. failure to forewarn the civilian population. For our purposes, the significance is in the almost complete absence of documentation on how the citizens of Hiroshima and Nagasaki suffered at the time and in the years following the events (in 1945 alone, hundreds of thousands of people—mostly civilians—are thought to have died as a result of both the initial blasts and consequent medical complications; the total number of deaths due to radiation-related illnesses in the years and decades thereafter is unknown). Given our analysis, the dearth of documentation of these events by the American media is exactly what we would predict from a national mass news media. People do not usually seek news that leads them to question the "goodness" of their own nation or makes them feel responsible for the large-scale suffering of others. Far more typically, they seek to see the events of the world in a way that validates their values and allegiances.

In a brief article in the *New York Times* (May 27, 2016),[2] which focused on U.S. President Barrack Obama's visit to Hiroshima, several Japanese survivors of the August 6, 1945 nuclear attack were interviewed on how they felt about Obama's visit, and about U.S. actions during World War II that led to the dropping of nuclear bombs on the people of Japan. Importantly, very few of the survivors' comments published in that article condemned the United States' decision to drop the bomb, while several comments implicated the interviewees' own country of Japan. Related

> What other points of view should be considered in reasoning through the problem being approached in the article? What are the strengths and weaknesses of these viewpoints? Am I fairmindedly considering the insights behind these viewpoints?

articles also played down the horrors in the atrocity; very little was said about the fact that, when visiting Japan to commemorate those who died in the war, President Obama did not intend to, and indeed did not, apologize for the killing of innocent people through use of nuclear weapons by the United States. Much was said in the president's speech about the general problem of war and of weapons that can cause so much destruction, but, again, no apology was given.

It does leave the reader to ponder what may have been conveniently left out of the U S. media reports on that particular piece of "news," since alternative news outlets and progressive war analysts have argued that dropping the bombs on Nagasaki and Hiroshima was unnecessary to stop the war (contrary to the publicly stated rationale of the United States at the time). For a well-reasoned view on this,

---

2   "Survivors Recount Horrors of Hiroshima and Nagasaki" (https://www.nytimes.com/2016/05/28/world/asia/survivors-recount-horrors-of-hiroshima-and-nagasaki.html).

read the "Interview with legendary whistleblower Daniel Ellsberg following his 89th arrest for resisting nuclear weapons, nuclear war and government secrecy, by Dennis Berstein, in Covert Action Magazine" (September 24, 2019).[3]

Again, the point is that those in the "home country" would rather avoid hearing of its own unethical behavior, even when that behavior occurred many years ago. The news media helps by glossing over unpleasant realities that would force us to face what we have done, and even to apologize. Through this facade, we can live in a fairytale world in which "we" are the virtuous victors by default, and those we harm naturally deserved it. (For a deeper understanding of how governments engage in unethical actions, work through *Think for Yourself 9: Identifying Unethical Government Actions* in Appendix A.)

HOW THE NEWS MEDIA FOSTER SOCIOCENTRIC THINKING

The key insight is this: the major media and press in all countries of the world present events in terms that presuppose or imply the "correctness" of the ideology (or ideologies) dominant in their respective countries. Our hope is not in changing the news media; news reporters and editors operate within a system of economic imperatives and constraints that dominate their work. Their audience is captive to an enculturated conception of the world.

As aspiring critical consumers of the mass media, we must learn to recognize that mainstream news is inevitably based on a sociocentric view of the world. We must learn how to recognize national and cultural bias. There is no reason to suppose that the ideology dominant in our culture is more accurate or insightful than that of any other. Supposing that one's own culture is exceptionally truthful in presenting its picture of the world is evidence not of insight, but rather of ethnocentrism (a form of sociocentrism). Sociocentrism is a fundamental characteristic of all countries and cultures, and news media function as unwitting agents of the resulting social conventions and taboos.

A Mutually Reinforcing Relationship

Sociocentrism	The Media
Social conventions, beliefs, taboos seen as "the only correct way to think and live"	Reflecting, reinforcing, and presupposing those conventions, beliefs, and taboos

---

3 See https://covertactionmagazine.com/index.php/2019/09/24/interview-with-legendary-whistleblower-daniel-ellsberg-following-his-89th-arrest-for-resisting-nuclear-weapons-nuclear-war-andgovernment-secrecy/.

Many examples of sociocentric thinking can be found in the mass media. The media are an inherent part of the culture within which they function. And remember, those in the media must "sell" their stories. To remain in business, their papers, news broadcasts, and magazines must be economically successful.

Because much of the thinking within any given culture is sociocentric in nature to begin with, the news media have little choice but to package what they produce within a sociocentric framework. The vehicles of large-scale social communication in a society inevitably serve that society and advance its self-image. Biased coverage is the rule, not the exception.

The mainstream news media around the world are thus biased toward their country's "allies," and prejudiced against their "enemies." They therefore present events occurring in the countries of their allies in as favorable a light as possible, highlighting their "positive" deeds while downplaying their negative ones. When generating news stories about their "enemies," the opposite treatment inevitably follows. Generating positive stories about the admirable characteristics of one's enemies is unacceptable. At the same time, negative stories about enemies

What are the complexities in the issues in this news story? Are these complexities adequately addressed by the journalist? Are any difficulties in the issue being ignored?

are often popular and are therefore routinely generated and highlighted. The ability of a news consumer to identify these biased stories in action and mentally "re-write" them with an opposing bias is a crucial critical thinking skill. With it, one sees slanted constructs everywhere in the news. And when one sees through the bias, its persuasive effect on the mind diminishes or disappears. (For a deeper understanding of how sociocentricity is promulgated in the news, work through *Think for Yourself 10: Identifying Sociocentric Thinking in the News* in Appendix A.)

CHAPTER 4

BECOME AN ASTUTE MEDIA CONSUMER

HOW TO OBTAIN USEFUL INFORMATION FROM PROPAGANDA AND TYPICAL NEWS STORIES

Obtaining useful information, even from propaganda and one-sided news stories, is possible, but only if one learns to read, hear, or view them critically. This means we must analyze these stories with a clear awareness of the points of view they embody, recognizing attempts to influence our thinking and beliefs. One must analyze them as one analyzes one side of a multi-sided argument. One-sided presentations are not the truth pure and simple, though they contain at least part of the truth, the part that supports the side in question. What is more, in standard news stories, something of the opposing point of view is sometimes mentioned (though usually deemphasized in the last few paragraphs of the story, or couched in terms of dismissal).

Critical readers recognize one-sidedness and seek out viewpoints that are dismissed or ignored by a given source. They also note which stories are highlighted and which are buried in the background.

Here are some key questions you should ask when analyzing and interpreting news stories:

- Who is the intended audience?
- What point of view is being privileged?
- What point(s) of view is (are) being dismissed or played down?
- How can I gain access to the point of view being negated (from those who most intelligently understand it)?
- Which stories are featured most prominently, and why?
- What information is "buried" in the article, and why?

(For a deeper understanding of how news story placement influences our reading of the news, work through *Think for Yourself 11: Analyzing News Story Placement* in Appendix A.)

STEPS IN BECOMING A CRITICAL CONSUMER OF THE NEWS

1. **Understand the basic agenda of "news story construction":**
   Always keep in mind that the ultimate purpose of mainstream "news story construction" is to sell "stories" for a profit to particular audiences (each with

particular beliefs, values, and prejudices). It is not to educate. It is not to be fair to all sides, since all sides are rarely represented in the target audience. To sell news stories to an audience, one must carefully assemble those stories in such a way as to engage intended readers, and to reinforce or validate their beliefs, values, prejudices, and worldview. Journalists typically come from those who share the beliefs, values, prejudices, and worldview of the intended audience. The slanting of the story is then achieved "naturally." Constructing news stories for an audience requires that one determine:

a) what the audience would consider a "story" (what they would, and would not, be interested in),

b) what about a story would be considered most relevant and what about it would be considered least relevant to the audience (and, therefore, what to play up and what to play down),

c) how to construct leads or headlines for a story (to create an initial definition for the reader),

d) how much space or time to give a particular story,

e) how to relate the story to other stories, and to the audience's picture of themselves and their world, and

f) how to tell the story so it sounds "professional" (objective and unbiased to the readers, a mere accounting of bare facts).

2. **Use your knowledge of the logic of "news story construction," first, to "deconstruct" stories in the news and then to "reconstruct" them imaginatively with alternative biases and slants.**

You become a critical consumer of the news media, first, by understanding the agendas of the news media, the criteria the news media use in constructing the news (deciding what a "story" is, what stories to cover, and how to cover them to get the highest ratings or keep people on their websites for as long as possible). Skilled consumers of the news learn how to identify and assess national, social, and political emphases and agendas. They learn how to read between the lines and imaginatively recast stories-as-told into alternative stories as they might have been told from other points of view.

3. **Learn how to redefine issues, access alternative sources (both within and outside the mainstream), put events into a historical perspective, and notice and assess assumptions and implications.**

Systematic questioning and assessment are crucial to the critical processing of media messages.

4. **Learn how to identify low-credibility stories by noticing vested interests** · **or mass emotion associated with content.**

Stories are least credible when the interests of the producer or receiver of a story are involved, or when the passions of a mass audience are involved (mass fear, anger, hatred, patriotism, etc.). When a nation is at war, for example, stories about the war told by the nation's mainstream press (including all explanations of it) are suspect, as all nations produce mass propaganda during war to build support for it. Stories about persons involved in taboo sexual acts (though these acts may be common in other societies or at different times in history) would be another such case, because the disgust or outrage experienced by the reader would command telling the story in such a way as to justify those reactions as reasonable (e.g., "Nudists Arrested," "Sexual Predator Condemned"). Stories that arouse mass passions are typically highly one-sided in nature and thus should have low credibility to those who think critically.

(For a deeper understanding of how to identify and analyze bias in the news, work through *Think for Yourself 12: Identifying and Analyzing Biased News Stories* in Appendix A.)

MEDIA AWARENESS OF MEDIA BIAS

To what extent are the news media aware of bias and propaganda in their own constructions? This question does not have a definitive answer. All journalists realize they are writing for an audience. It doesn't follow, however, that they have thought through the implications of this, although some journalists are certainly much more aware of their own biases than others.

In the United States, Israel is a favored ally, so mistreatment or abuse of the Palestinians by the Israelis is usually covered under the idea of "justified reprisal." Because Fidel Castro of Cuba was always viewed within the United States as an enemy, mainstream news writers routinely presented Castro and Cuba in a negative light, ignoring or explaining away any achievement of the Cuban government (such as universal medical coverage and a low infant mortality rate). If and when persons in the news media recognize patterns of news coverage such as these, they must be careful in writing about them—lest they themselves be guilty of "irresponsible" and "biased" reporting.

> What point of view is being privileged in this news story? What points of view are being dismissed or played down?

Yet, as mentioned, in the past decade or more, the concept of advocacy journalism has taken root and become the prevalent form of journalism; accordingly, many journalists now do not at all aspire to be objective, but rather to advance the agendas of the group (political or otherwise) for which they are writing. They see their role as highlighting and advancing the goals of their readers and their leaders rather than engaging in even-handed journalism.

SENSITIVITY TO ADVERTISERS

Every group within a culture is not equally important to the news media. National media are, of course, biased in favor of national culture, religion, dominant beliefs, and social values. But within any complex culture, some groups play a more powerful role than others within media logic. For example, most news media profit comes from advertisers. These advertisers are not pleased if they, or the interests they represent, are cast in a bad light by the media they finance. News media, therefore, often avoid generating stories that negatively feature major advertisers. Put another way: because news media outlets can select from among a large mass of potential stories, and cannot carry more than a small percentage of what is available, they naturally, all other things being equal, choose to avoid or play down stories irritating to their advertisers. There are, of course, exceptions to this pattern. A lot depends on the "splash" the story would make or whether it is already "out."

Further, online news sources funded by advertising depend on a business model wherein consumers are kept engaged long enough to view advertisements. Again, this engagement can be maintained by telling people what they want to hear (regardless of whether it's important, relevant, or accurate), or producing content that entertains or outrages more than it informs. Advertisers can also influence what is reported or how, and may even withdraw their advertisements when the content of reporting is disagreeable to them or runs counter to their goals.[1]

Consider the following remarks focused on whether it is possible for the media to be objective, fair, and impartial in today's media climate (Atkins, 2016):

> Michelle Ciulla Lipkin, executive director of the National Association for Media Literacy Education (NAMLE), believes that "it's not possible given the financial model of media. They tell a story in a certain way to get viewers. With all the pressure, there's no ability to be objective. It's sad that news outlets are moneymaking entities. You're supposed to tell people information, not depend on ad sales. It's a cycle with the pressure to stay number one, to bring money in, and to be powerful. (p. 250)

SENSITIVITY TO POLITICIANS AND THE GOVERNMENT

National news media are always sensitive to the power of government. For one, national governments typically license and regulate news media by law. For another, much national news is "given" to news media through high governmental officials and agencies.

---

1   For detailed articles on this, see: https://doi.org/10.1007/s10551-012-1353-z, https://www.tandfonline.com/doi/abs/10.2753/JOA0091-3367360208, and https://journals.sagepub.com/doi/abs/10.1177/107769909106800118.

For these reasons, news media personnel hesitate to criticize the national government in certain fundamental ways. For example, if the national government names some other group or nation as an enemy, the national news media generally present that group or nation as unfavorably as they can. If the government attacks another nation militarily, the national news media typically line up behind the government like cheerleaders at a sporting event. The news media are characteristically apologists for the policies and acts of the national government.

An exception to this occurs when elements in the national news media are linked to a political party not presently in power. Their protection then comes from the power and interests represented by the opposition party. They are in such cases beholden to the views and beliefs of their political supporters. In the United States, particular news outlets are now frequently more influenced by the Democratic or Republican Parties, but both parties tend to unite around the same basic worldview and beliefs of the broader society. Both tend to identify the same countries as friends or enemies; both are responsive to major economic forces and concentrations of wealth and power.

> Who is the intended audience for this story?

The basic logic is always the same. The media are presenting the news within a point of view. The point of view represents interests affecting media profitability and deeply entrenched in social ideology. The news media always focus on profit, though that focus is obscured and kept in the background.

(For a deeper understanding of how news outlets frequently cater to government inappropriately, work through *Think for Yourself 13: Identifying News Stories That Pander to the Government* in Appendix A.)

SENSITIVITY TO POWERFUL INTERESTS

News media sources try to maximize their profit while minimizing costs. Investigative journalism is more expensive than pre-packaged stories (news from press releases, news conferences, speeches, etc.). Realizing that their position of power within the culture is threatened if they fail to maintain a favorable public image, powerful economic interests continually invest in marketing their respective images to the public, not only through massive advertising but also through press releases and stories pitched to the press. There is therefore a symbiotic relationship between powerful media sources (which need news stories) and powerful economic interests (which generate and disseminate news stories to their benefit). This is true in virtually all nations.

All human organizations with significant influence (gained primarily through money and political connections) work to shape the daily news in their interests, including:

- Powerful industries such as technology, manufacturing, communications, agriculture, weapons producers, airlines, the criminal justice industry (including prisons, police, lawyers, social workers, and prison contractors), construction, banking, auto, insurance, public relations and advertising, broadcasting, and entertainment.
- Governmental agencies and persons in positions of power in the executive, legislative, judicial, military, and intelligence communities.
- Religious groups, professional groups, unions, and other groups organized around vested interests.

From the Great Depression in the 1930s through World War II and the beginning of the Cold War in the 1950s, reporters seemed to reflect establishment views more often than they exposed the failings and foibles of the powerful. They seldom challenged government news management or the press agentry of private business and the entertainment industry (Downie & Kaiser, 2002, p. 10). Of course, exceptions can occur, for instance, when the government acts in egregious ways and happens also not to be of the same political affiliation as the media producer.

(For a deeper understanding of how news outlets frequently pander to business interests, work through *Think for Yourself 14: Identifying Stories That Favor Business Interests* in Appendix A.)

SENSITIVITY TO THEIR COMPETITORS

News media run stories in light of the news as presented by other media outlets. When mainstream news outlets treat a story as "big," the others typically pick it up so as not to be viewed as deficient in coverage. Mainstream media tend to move as one herd, slavishly following their leaders. In other words, national and international coverage differ very little from one news outlet to another within any given country—except, of course, where partisan politics are at play. The growing trend of advocacy journalism, usually through the lens of politics, as not only acceptable, but even to be expected or the norm, has to some degree changed the terrain of competition and therefore of coverage. However, it has not changed the problems inherent in news outlets "keeping up with the competition" by covering many of the same stories as one another, often in a similar manner (especially when politics is excluded).

(For a deeper understanding of how news outlets cover the news in ways both similar to and different from one another, work through *Think for Yourself 15: Analyzing News Outlets for Similarities and Differences* in Appendix A.)

THE BIAS TOWARD NOVELTY AND SENSATIONALISM

The "news" typically is constructed with a systematic bias in favor of reporting what is novel, bizarre, sensational, or odd. What happens every day—no matter how intrinsically important—is often sacrificed. But great social problems typically are embedded in day-to-day events that are repeated thousands, millions, or billions of times. Such events are often not dramatic or odd, but pathetically common. On the one hand, if a large bank systematically overcharges millions of customers a small amount of money, it succeeds in stealing millions of dollars. Yet, such a practice may not be considered news. If a solitary bank robber makes off with $10,000, on the other hand, it will likely make the news. If millions of children are bullied in schools every day,

> How can I gain access to the point of view being negated in this news story by seeking alternative news sources (from those who most intelligently understand it)?

and consequently suffer lifelong damage, this problem is usually not considered news. But if two children are caught playing "doctor" at school, that may well be considered news. If millions of children go to bed hungry every night all over the globe, that is not news. But if one school serves caviar during lunch, that is news. If women and children are sold every day in an international slave trade, that is not necessarily news; but if a solitary teacher has a sexual relationship with a student, that is news.

(For a deeper understanding of the role sensationalism plays in the news, work through *Think for Yourself 16: Identifying Sensationalism in the News* in Appendix A.)

CRITICAL CONSUMERS OF THE NEWS

Manipulating critical consumers of the news is difficult because:

- They study alternative perspectives and worldviews, learning how to interpret events from multiple viewpoints.
- They seek understanding and insight through multiple sources of thought and information, not simply those of the mainstream media.
- They learn how to identify the viewpoints embedded in news stories.
- They mentally rewrite (reconstruct) news stories through awareness of how stories would be told from multiple perspectives.
- They analyze news constructs in the same way they analyze other representations of reality (as some blend of fact and interpretation).
- They assess news stories for their clarity, accuracy, relevance, depth, breadth, and significance.

- They notice contradictions and inconsistencies in the news (often within the same story).
- They notice the agenda and interests served by a story.
- They notice the facts covered and the facts ignored.
- They notice when what is represented as fact that is actually in dispute.
- They notice questionable assumptions implicit in stories.
- They notice what is implied (but not openly stated).
- They notice which implications are ignored and which are emphasized.
- They notice which points of view are systematically put into a favorable light and which in an unfavorable light.
- They mentally correct stories reflecting bias toward the unusual, the dramatic, and the sensational by putting them into perspective or discounting them.
- They question the social conventions and taboos being used to define issues and problems.
- They are careful not to be overly influenced by advocacy journalism.
- They do not get their news from social media sites, but rather seek news from reputable sources.
- They avoid melodrama and sensationalism in the news.

(For a deeper understanding of how the news can be written in different ways, work through *Think for Yourself 17: Rewrite a News Story* in Appendix A.)

DOMINANT AND DISSENTING VIEWS: FINDING ALTERNATIVE SOURCES OF INFORMATION

To find sources of information supporting the dominant views within a culture is easy. The problem for most of us is finding well-thought-through views that question mainstream news sources. In countries where the government controls the news, for example, it is hard to gain access to views that critique the government. Only a minority of thinkers are motivated to look beyond the dominant views by digging beneath the surface and bringing forward what is unpleasant or painful to the majority (or damaging to the party line). *Insightful critiques of a society within that society are typically hard to come by,* and where they appear, they are often dismissed out of hand (by the majority, who are engaging in it) rather than considered thoughtfully.

Of course, the main point is that every society in the world today has multiple (sometimes divergent) mainstream and dissenting views. And it is important to recognize that we are not saying that dissenting views are correct and mainstream views are incorrect; there are insights to be gained from all major conflicting worldviews. What is most important is to locate both mainstream and dissenting views *expressed in their most articulate and insightful forms*. In other words, the ideal approach to studying any important issue is to access a full range of views as expressed by their most skilled and insightful defenders.

One faces two challenges: 1) to locate a full range of views on multilogical issues, and 2) to locate well-informed, fairminded spokespersons for each major position in the spectrum.

Let us look at the United States. American mainstream views can be found in any of a large number of major American news outlets (*New York Times, Washington Post, Baltimore Sun, Boston Globe, Chicago Tribune, Plain Dealer* in Cleveland, *Los Angeles Times, Star Tribune* in Minneapolis, *Philadelphia Inquirer, Sacramento Bee, San Francisco Chronicle*, and so on). Similar lists of mainstream news outlets could be produced for every country in the world. Of course, there would be some overlap in viewpoints between mainstream newspapers from various nations and cultures, depending on the extent to which they share religious views, economic interests, and political traditions. Locating dissenting views within nations and cultures is more difficult, depending on the extent to which dissenters are forced to go "underground." The best general source for the views of important dissenters is through the scholarly magazines and presses of the world. In some cases, one can locate publications dealing with issues in greater depth than the mainstream news.

> Which stories are featured most prominently, and why? Which news stories are buried or ignored, and why?

In the United States, for example, *The Nation* is one such publication. From its conception in 1865, it has provided an outlet for intellectually dissenting points of view. Its contributors have included Nelson Algren, Hannah Arendt, W. H. Auden, James Baldwin, Willa Cather, Emily Dickinson, John Dos Passos, W. E. B. Du Bois, Albert Einstein, Lawrence Ferlinghetti, Robert Frost, Carlos Fuentes, Emma Goldman, Langston Hughes, Henry James, Martin Luther King, Jr., D. H. Lawrence, Robert Lowell, Tomas Mann, H. L. Mencken, Arthur Miller, Pablo Neruda, Octavio Paz, Sylvia Plath, Ezra Pound, Bertrand Russell, Jean Paul Sartre, Upton Sinclair, Wallace Stevens, I. F. Stone, Gore Vidal, Kurt Vonnegut, Alice Walker, and William Butler Yeats. Clearly, this is a valuable source for non-mainstream points of view. In addition to providing a weekly magazine on controversial political and cultural issues, *The Nation* has also established a Digital Archive covering 7,000 weekly issues.[2]

Of course, all sources of news and commentary should be read critically, carefully analyzed and assessed, and used as vehicles for intellectual independence, as sources for *part* of the truth, not as vehicles of "THE TRUTH." The ideal is freedom from any single, or narrow, point of view or perspective.

---

2   See www.thenation.com/archive.

BURIED, IGNORED, OR UNDERREPORTED STORIES

Of the millions of events that take place in the world on any given day, only a tiny percentage of them—perhaps a few hundred—are made into "news" stories (for a given culture) within mainstream news outlets. Again, the stories selected typically confirm the dominant cultural viewpoint of the society. Stories that disconfirm the dominant cultural viewpoint are ignored, underreported, or "buried" (given little coverage and attention). Stories buried in the reporting of one culture, however, may be front-page news in the reporting of another.

This phenomenon is intensified when there is conflict between cultures. In such cases, when the same events are covered, they are conceptualized very differently. For example, in wartime, each side tells the story of the conflict to its home audience in self-serving terms. Hence, though both sides commit atrocities, each side's mainstream media highlight mainly the atrocities of the enemy, while suppressing, denying, or minimizing their own government's atrocities. Each side conceptualizes itself as representing the forces of good (decency, justice, and so on) and its enemies as representing the forces of evil. The predictability of this self-serving function of mass media is highlighted in research into the mutual "image of the enemy":

> Enemy-images mirror each other—that is, each side attributes the same virtues to itself and the same vices to the enemy. "We" are trustworthy, peace-loving, honorable, and humanitarian; "they" are treacherous, warlike, and cruel. In surveys of Americans conducted in 1942, the first five adjectives chosen to characterize both Germans and Japanese (enemies) included warlike, and cruel, none of which appeared among the first five describing the Russians (allies); in 1966 all three had disappeared from American characterizations of the Germans and Japanese (allies), but now the Russians (no longer allies, although more rivals than enemies) were warlike and treacherous. . . . The enemy-image acts like a distorting lens, which overemphasizes information that confirms it and filters out information incompatible with it. Thus the mass media play up incidents of an enemy's treachery or cruelty, and ignore examples of humanitarian or honorable behavior. (Jerome Frank, *Chemtech*, August 1982, p. 467)

(For a deeper understanding of how mainstream news outlets tend to ignore important stories, work through *Think for Yourself 18: Identifying Ignored and Important Stories* in Appendix A.)

HOW THE INTERNET AND OTHER TECHNOLOGIES PERVADE OUR LIVES

To effectively navigate and participate in the world today, it is necessary to understand how the internet works, and, more broadly, how technologies affect our lives. The internet has become an essential tool and information source for the average person living today. Moreover, technological advances in the past half-century have thrust most people across the world into a highly technical and complex world that they have no choice but to navigate.

Without basic critical thinking abilities, it is impossible to comprehend and properly assess the internet, the news embedded in it, and, more broadly, the technologies surrounding us. We need to look closely at how the internet works. We need to know how technologies are on one hand improving, and on the other hand diminishing, the quality of our lives. We need to understand the big picture of technology—to both better protect ourselves and to think critically about the technologies we support and participate in.

It is essential to understand, at the outset, that the websites and technologies being created for us are only as good as the reasoning that conceptualizes, creates, and maintains them over time. By this we mean specifically the reasoning of the people overseeing and executing a given website or technology. In many cases, if the reasoning used in the development process is limited in some important dimensions, products are created that the public is then forced into buying, because those are the only such products available to

What information is "buried" in the article, and why?

them. A primary assumption that should be questioned, then, is that the people creating the technologies are also experts in understanding how the end-user will want and need to use that technology. For instance, a small number of companies monopolize the design and development of cell phones. Over time, to keep us buying, these phones become more complex with added features (often of little or no use to most buyers), while at the same time losing desirable features from a previous version of the same phone.

This points up the underlying pervasive authority of money on the fabric of human life, and specifically the untenable pattern of constantly spending on products for the purpose of maintaining the current capitalistic system, which is designed so that it can never be satiated no matter how productive our output. This way of living requires the pursuit of ever higher yields of money through the ramping up of capitalism across the world, and is manifest in companies constantly creating products with as short a life span as we will tolerate, which can then be thrown away and replaced as soon as possible. This enables companies to force us into purchasing new technologies as soon as possible in order to constantly fill their coffers. Never mind that many of these products are far inferior to products made (in some cases) a hundred or more years ago. Never mind that the earth's resources are being continually diminished and our trash heaps are ever growing.

HOW THE INTERNET WORKS: THE BIG PICTURE

To understand the logic of the internet is first to see it as a huge information-propagating machine, with tentacles going out into countless directions which, in the perceivable future, will continue to expand into something like infinity. For our purposes, we need not catalog these tentacles (whose vastness would exhaust the mind, as well as become obsolete as soon as they were cataloged). Rather, what we need is to grasp *the logic of the whole* and how critical thinking can help us weave our way through internet information sources, weed out junk and nonsense unworthy of our attention, and focus on what is best and what enhances, rather than diminishes, the quality of our lives.

First and foremost, as with all creations of humans, we must recognize that every website, again, is a product of human reasoning; even if generated by machines, every website must be at some point conceived by human reasoning, if only to set it in motion. As such, every website should be judged according to the *quality of reasoning* embedded in it. See in Chapter 2 an introduction to the elements of reasoning and

> Can I imaginatively reconstruct the story from a different, perhaps more reasonable viewpoint?

other basic critical thinking concepts that will help you better navigate the internet without being taken to websites against your interest.

Here are some simple starting places:

1. For most people today, spending enormous amounts of time on the internet is considered both natural and good. However, critical thinkers limit their exposure to the internet to those information sources and sites that enhance some part of their real lives. They spend far less time online than the vast majority of people, who seem or are addicted to the internet. This is because virtual reality simply is not the same as living in and experiencing the real world. Virtual reality can never replace the beauty and dynamism of experiencing actual human relationships face to face. For the most part, "succeeding" on the internet is not the same as succeeding in the real world—the latter of which entails developing individual skills of creativity. Consider, for instance, the time wasted on gaming. Or consider the fact that people "play instruments" such as the guitar online, believing themselves to be actual musicians when they are nothing of the kind. These endeavors give the *illusion of success*, but in fact are *addictions of the mind* that lead away from engaging in real-life healthy and creative activities such as sports or playing the actual guitar or piano. Those who fall prey to these types of illusions are typically unaware of the fact that algorithms are designed, increasingly with the help of psychologists, to figure out exactly how to keep people addicted to these games and other digital activities.

2. Recognize that we can divide internet content into two basic (but often overlapping) categories:

   a) the websites you choose to visit and activities you choose to engage in.

   b) the things that come at you and happen to you as byproducts of visiting these websites—the advertisements bombarding you, advertisers tracking you in ways you are unaware of, government surveillance systems, and so forth.

The varieties of websites you can choose to visit are ever expanding, so we won't try to catalogue them all, but here are some basic types:

1. **Social networking sites** such as Facebook, Twitter, Instagram, Snapchat, and LinkedIn—these are place where people talk about and share all manner of things, including what is frequently termed "news."

2. **Shopping** sites, such as the monstrous Amazon and numerous smaller sites, where you can purchase things that come right to your door.

3. **Educational** and other information-propagating websites, such as encyclopedias; video-streaming services; schools, colleges, and universities (public and private, professional and technical, musical, artistic, and so on); podcasts; and audio book sites.

4. **Gaming sites,** including instrument and sports simulations.

5. **Social casinos,** where people pretend they are gambling. Users are not winning real money, but they are paying real money to play. In fact, many people are apparently now addicted to the "game" of gambling in ways similar to additions to actual gambling, some of whom have lost tens of thousands of dollars or more at these social casinos.[3]

6. **News** sites, including mainstream and alternative news.

7. **Membership** sites, including academic and technical sites, or sites dedicated to arts or the professions. Some of these are private and require payment to join.

ASSESS A GIVEN WEBSITE USING CRITICAL THINKING STANDARDS

Any website must be individually assessed for quality, since no standards are built into the internet. Freedom of speech allows for even the most inane, crass, immature, and dangerous thoughts to be broadcast, and people with similar biases tend to share their biased "news" and commentary with one another, validating their already narrowminded views.

---

3 To understand some of the important implications of this, read how Facebook works with social casinos to keep people addicted: https://www.revealnews.org/article/if-you-have-an-addiction-youre-screwed -how-facebook-and-social-casinos-target-the-vulnerable/.

Again, the quality of information—and, indeed, everything—found on the internet is only as good as the quality of the thinking that gives rise to it. And since the quality of human thinking is typically ignored in human societies, we can't expect any given website to be at all concerned with advancing reasonable principles.

Use the critical thinking tools laid out in Chapter 2 when assessing any website for quality.

USING THE INTERNET IN SEEKING THE NEWS

The internet can be used to locate both mainstream and dissenting views from virtually any country in the world. Below are three sources we have located for non-mainstream viewpoints. As always, we do not offer sources as "THE TRUTH," but as aids in obtaining alternatives to the content of mainstream media news.

In some cases, particularly in countries where those with dissenting views are put in prison or killed, dissenting views must be sought from expatriates rather than from resident citizens.

Amnesty International (www.amnesty.org) is a good source for discovering persons whose views are being forcibly suppressed. According to their website, the organization works with the news media to expose human rights abuses and documents stories focused on uncovering major human rights issues.[4]

A second example of the sort of important resource one can locate on the internet is Statewatch. Statewatch serves as a watchdog organization and database whose goal is to monitor state and civil liberties in Europe. To get a sense of its thoroughness, Statewatch has compiled more than 34,000 entries in its database since 1991, containing news features, sources, and reports.[5]

A third example is *Covert Action Magazine* whose goal is to document the involvement of intelligence agencies in actions violating human rights, as well as international and national laws. This alternative news outlet documents acts that are usually "disowned" by intelligence agencies in the countries sponsoring them. *Covert Action* reporters' sources are typically investigative journalists, professors, and scholars.[6]

Another strategy is to search the internet under descriptors such as "Japanese perspectives," "Asian perspectives," "Chinese perspectives," "African perspectives," "Central American perspectives," "South American perspectives," or "Islamic Perspectives." This should help you locate a range of cultural and political standpoints.

---

4   For news from Amnesty International, see https://www.amnestyusa.org/news/.

5   Visit www.statewatch.org.

6   See covertactionmagazine.org.

ADDITIONAL ALTERNATIVE NEWS SOURCES

Below are some non-mainstream sources of news, as well as sources of background information for the news. We assume you will read these sources with the same criticality we are recommending for mainstream views. Once again, we do not offer these sources as "THE TRUTH" but, instead, as helpful non-mainstream viewpoints providing alternatives to the content of mainstream media news. See if you can add others to this list.

Project Censored
www.projectcensored.org

Free Speech TV
www.Freespeech.org

Harpers
www.harpers.org

In These Times
www.inthesetimes.com

The Progressive
www.progressive.org

Z Magazine
www.zcomm.org

CounterPunch
www.counterpunch.org

AlterNet
www.alternet.org

Common Dreams
www.commondreams.org

Mother Jones
www.motherjones.com

Independent Media Center
www.indymedia.org

Dollars and Sense
www.dollarsandsense.org

The Nation
www.thenation.com

Center for Investigative Reporting
www.revealnews.org

READINGS THAT HELP YOU BECOME A MORE INDEPENDENT THINKER

To detect bias and propaganda in the news media requires a commitment to thinking for oneself. The process of becoming an independent thinker is furthered significantly by reading the writings of important dissenters, thinkers who questioned mainstream views and who thought outside the cultural box. Each person listed below is considered by scholars to represent high-level dissent. They are acclaimed

> Does the journalist represent relevant viewpoints in good faith?

as classic authors due to the importance of their thoughts and the universal nature of their insights (i.e., their importance and relevance across time and culture). Of course there are many others, but this is a starting place.

Thomas Paine (*Common Sense*, 1776)

William Lloyd Garrison (*The Journal of the Times and The Liberator*, 1831)

Wendell Phillips (*Speeches, Lectures, and Letters*, 1863)

Margaret Fuller (*Memoirs* [2 volumes], 1852)

Henry David Thoreau (*Essay on Civil Disobedience*, 1849)

John Stuart Mill (*On Liberty*, 1859)

Emma Goldman (*My Disillusionment with Russia*, 1923)

Henry George (*Social Problems*, 1883)

Thorstein Veblen (*The Vested Interests and the Common Man*, 1919)

John Peter Altgeld (*Our Penal Machinery and Its Victims*, 1884)

Lincoln Steffens (*The Struggle for Self-Government*, 1906)

William Graham Sumner (*Folkways*, 1906)

Gustavus Myers (*History of the Great American Fortunes* [2 volumes], 1907)

José Ortega y Gasset (*The Revolt of the Masses*, 1932)

William J. Lederer (*A Nation of Sheep*, 1961)

H. L. Mencken (*Prejudices* [6 volumes], 1977)

Eric Fromm (*To Have or to Be*, 1976)

Eric Hoffer (*The True Believer*, 1951)

Matthew Josephson (*The Robber Barons*, 1962)

Bertrand Russell (*Unpopular Essays*, 1952)

C. Wright Mills (*The Power Elite*, 1959)

Howard Zinn (*A People's History of the United States*, 1995)

Ralph Nader (*The Ralph Nader Reader*, 2000)

Noam Chomsky (*Manufacturing Consent: The Political Economy of the Mass Media*, 2002)

Bill Moyers (*Moyers on Democracy*, 2008)

CHAPTER 5

THE FUTURE OF THE NEWS

IS IT POSSIBLE FOR THE NEWS MEDIA TO REFORM?

To provide the public with non-biased writing, journalists around the world would have to, first, enter empathically into worldviews to which they are not sympathetic at present. They would have to imagine writing for audiences that hold views antithetical to the ones they hold. They would have to develop insights into their own sociocentrism. They would have to do the things we have suggested are done by critical consumers of the news.

Imagine Israeli journalists writing articles that present the Palestinian point of view sympathetically. Imagine Pakistani journalists writing articles that present the Indian point of view sympathetically.

The most basic point is this: Journalists do not determine the nature and demands of their jobs. They do not determine what their readers want, think, hate, or fear. The

> How would the news be presented in fairminded critical societies?

nature and demands of their job are determined by the broader nature of societies themselves and the beliefs, values, and worldviews of its members. It is human nature to see the world, in the first instance, in egocentric and sociocentric terms. Most people are not interested in having their minds broadened. They want their present beliefs and values extolled and confirmed. Like football fans, they want the "home team" to win, and when it wins, to triumph gloriously. If it loses, they want to be told the game wasn't important, or the other side cheated, or the officials were biased against them. As long as the overwhelming mass of persons in the broader society are drawn to news articles that reinforce, and do not question, their fundamental views or passions, the economic imperatives will remain the same. The logic is parallel to that of reforming a nation's eating habits. As long as the mass of people want unhealthy processed foods, the market will sell unhealthy processed foods to them. And as long as the mass of people want simplistic news articles that reinforce egocentric and sociocentric thinking, which present the world in sweeping terms of good and evil (with the readers' views and passions treated as good, and those of the readers' conceived enemies as evil), the news media will generate such articles for them. The profits and ratings of news sources, with their fingers on the pulse of their readers and viewers, will continue to soar.

(To further explore the question: Is it reasonable to expect the mainstream news media to reform? Work through *Think for Yourself 19: Can the Media Reform?* in Appendix A.)

IS THE EMERGENCE OF A "CRITICAL SOCIETY" POSSIBLE?

In 1906, in a concluding chapter of his classic book, *Folkways*, William Graham Sumner raised the possibility of the development of "critical" societies, by which he meant societies that adopt critical thinking as an essential part of their way of life. Sumner recognized that critical thinking "is our only guarantee against delusion, deception, superstition, and misapprehension of ourselves and our earthly circumstances." He recognized education as "good just so far as it produces a well-developed critical faculty." He states:

> The critical habit of thought, if usual in a society, will pervade all its mores, because it is a way of taking up the problems of life. People educated in it cannot be stampeded . . . are slow to believe. They can hold things as possible or probable in all degrees, without certainty and without pain. They can wait for evidence and weigh evidence, uninfluenced by the emphasis or confidence with which assertions are made on one side or the other. They can resist appeals to their dearest prejudices and all kinds of cajolery. Education in the critical faculty is the only education of which it can be truly said that it makes good citizens.

No country or culture in the world routinely fosters education as perceived by Sumner. As things now stand, such education is the rare exception in any society. The detection of bias and propaganda in the news media is possible only for those willing to be diligent in pursuing news from multiple sources representing multiple alternative cultural and national standpoints. It is possible only for those who—in their reading and thinking and judging—are willing to swim against the tide.

---

20 Barriers to Critical Societies

To illustrate the fact that we as humans tend not to take thinking seriously in today's cultures, consider the following 20 barriers to critical societies.

Most people:

1. are only superficially aware of critical thinking.
2. cannot clearly articulate the ideal of critical thinking, know of it only as a positive buzz term, and, in any case, habitually violate its standards, and in multiple ways. Most humans, in other words, have not aspired to the ideal of critical thought, and most who have done so (having only an implicit idea of it) have succeeded only modestly.
3. uncritically accept the traditional, mainstream views and beliefs of their culture.
4. are "culture bound" (enslaved within social conventions).
5. uncritically accept the views of authority figures.

6. are not aware of, and do not attempt to explicitly use, intellectual standards in their thinking.

7. do not understand human thinking (their own or others') or the impediments to reasonability.

8. (unconsciously) believe much that is arbitrary or irrational.

9. uncritically accept bureaucratic rules, procedures, and formulas.

10. accept a variety of forms of authoritarianism (such as blindly following a religious ideology).

11. are uncreative and unoriginal.

12. are trapped in their social class.

13. never come to think well within any subject, and have no sense of what it is to think beyond subject-matter compartments.

14. do not believe in freedom of thought and speech, or in a wide range of other inalienable freedoms.

15. are biased on questions of gender, culture, species, and politics.

16. use their intellects only superficially.

17. have little command over their primitive emotions and desires; rather, they tend to be at the mercy of their own irrational impulses and passions.

18. do not value true spontaneity, naturalness, or artlessness.

19. are unable and/or unwilling to think within the viewpoints of others who hold a different worldview.

20. are unable to achieve self-actualization, self-command, or enlightenment, because they lack command of their thoughts and understanding of the relationship between thoughts and emotions.

(For a deeper understanding of fairminded critical societies and how the world would be different were we to value fairminded critical thinking across human cultures, work through *Think for Yourself 20: Imagining a Critical Society and Its Implications* in Appendix A.)

CONCLUSION

> To what degree does my country embody the principles of fairminded critical thinking?

Learning to detect media bias and propaganda in the national and world news is an art that takes extended time to develop. Yet it is also an art essential to intellectual responsibility, integrity, and freedom. This book presents a starting place for the development of intellectual analysis and assessment applied to news stories. As one develops in this art, one experiences a progressive shedding of layers of social indoctrination, ethnocentrism, and sociocentrism.

In the end, of course, each of us must decide for ourselves what to believe and how to act. We can do this critically or uncritically, rationally or irrationally, and egocentrically or fairmindedly. We can either tacitly accept our social conditioning and its accompanying ideology, or we can make a deliberative, conscious choice to grow beyond that conditioning. The choice is ours; no one can legitimately make it for us. If we choose to go beyond our social conditioning and think for ourselves, we can become free persons and conscientious citizens.

> Is it possible for the news media to reform, given the problem of vested interest, egocentricity and group think?

APPENDIX A

THINK FOR YOURSELF ACTIVITIES

In various places in the book, we refer to the following activities. Beside each one is the page number where you can find the related content. By working through these activities, you can better internalize the points being made in the book.

Think for Yourself 1: Targeting Political Journalism (for the relevant content, refer to pages 7–8)

Identify three news outlets that function primarily as a voice for a given politician or political party. What news stories exemplify your position? Have you looked at just one side of the political spectrum, or are you considering more than one side? Do you find yourself seeking news outlets and examples primarily on the political side you disagree with, or are you open-mindedly considering looking for bias on "your side" of the political spectrum?

Think for Yourself 2 : Identify Accusations of Spreading Fake News (for the relevant content, refer to page 15)

Identify several cases in which one media outlet accuses another of the spreading of fake news. Examine and assess these accusations based on standards of critical thinking. For instance, are these accusations *accurate* or *logical*? Has *sufficient* information been included, or has some important information been deliberately left out in order to distort the news, thereby advancing one's own position dishonestly? How can you dig deeper to learn what in fact is going on, to figure out what is being hidden or distorted, and precisely why?

Think for Yourself 3: Identifying Irrational Lenses and Their Consequences (for the relevant content, refer to page 36)

How might the irrational lenses in your own mind affect the way you perceive the news? How might such lenses influence the news sources you consider most important and valuable?

Think for Yourself 4: Contrasting Worldviews (for the relevant content, refer to pages 43–44)

Are you familiar with any worldview that contrasts with the worldview of your culture? If so, what are some important similarities and differences between the beliefs of your culture and those of a different culture? If not, see whether you can locate a characterization of one worldview that contrasts with the worldview of your home culture. For example, if you see the world from the perspective of a North American "Christian" culture, accumulate some information about the perspective of a Middle Eastern "Muslim" culture. Find a news source on the internet that provides coverage of world events from that alternative cultural perspective. Note some differences you find in the same events being covered in contrasting ways. See whether you can notice your prejudices in favor of your home culture.

Think for Yourself 5: Identifying the Promotion of Irrational Viewpoints Disguised as Rational Ones (for the relevant content, refer to pages 44–46)

Identify some examples of one or more news outlets advancing hatred or some other irrational beliefs as a rational perspective.

What irrational beliefs are these news outlets advancing, and how are they justifying their slanted treatment of the news?

Think for Yourself 6: Identifying the Interests of Readers (for the relevant content, refer to page 47)

Analyze the main page of an internet news site to identify the viewpoint of the paper's primary audience. See whether you can figure out what the readers of that news outlet think is important. How would you characterize the readers' primary viewpoints? How do they see the world? What do they want to read about? What would they rather not read about?

Think for Yourself 7: Identifying News Outlets That Exemplify Fairminded, Multidimensional Thinking (for the relevant content, refer to pages 49–50)

Identify one or more news outlets you believe come closest to fitting the criteria outlined for news writers and outlets that embody fairminded, multidimensional thinking. You will gain more from this exercise if you identify at least one such outlet that tends to take a different perspective from your own on current affairs.

For each news outlet you identify, give an example that illuminates the best reasoning on all important sides of the issue.

Think for Yourself 8: Exploring Propaganda in the News (for the relevant content, refer to pages 51–53)

Identify one or more news websites that seem to blatantly spread propaganda. What stories found at this site support your position? Contrast this with one or more news sites less prone to propaganda.

Think for Yourself 9: Identifying Unethical Government Actions (for the relevant content, refer to pages 53–55)

Identify a news story, either from the mainstream news or from an alternative news source, that focuses on one or more ethical wrongdoings sanctioned by your government or culture—i.e., actions that people within your country would like to avoid knowing or thinking about. Identify the reason(s) people would like to avoid thinking about the issue. How is the wrongdoing treated? Is it highlighted, or is it hidden?

Think for Yourself 10: Identifying Sociocentric Thinking in the News (for the relevant content, refer to pages 55–56)

Locate one news story exemplifying the fact that reporters, as a rule, uncritically accept the social conventions and taboos of their culture. For example, it is not uncommon to read U.S. mainstream news editorials in which women are depicted as fearful of looking "old" as they age, and therefore resort to all manner of drastic and expensive measures to appear younger, including Botox and elaborate surgical procedures. Romantic relationships between movie stars also seem of interest to people as "news," especially when there is a considerable difference in age. These types of stories appear frequently because they represent cultural conventions.

Think for Yourself 11: Analyzing News Story Placement (for the relevant content, refer to page 57)

Read through the homepage of a nationally recognized news website. Find examples of relatively unimportant but highlighted articles. Contrast these with examples of more important stories (e.g., hidden amidst other pages on the site, or toward the bottom of the homepage, or appearing in smaller font). For instance, the *New York Times* usually focuses its homepage on national news and editorials of mixed quality, often from their regular journalists, at the expense of important international stories and pressing environmental reports and often leaving out more scholarly view.

Think for Yourself 12: Identifying and Analyzing Biased News Stories (for the relevant content, refer to pages 57–59)

Locate a news story on a major news website that appears biased or is told from a slanted view. Identify:

1. The bias(es) inherent in the story.
2. The viewpoints that are ignored or distorted.

   Then figure out how the story would have to be constructed if it were to fairly represent all relevant viewpoints.

Think for Yourself 13: Identifying News Stories That Pander to the Government (for the relevant content, refer to pages 60–61)

Identify a news story in which one or both of the following are true:

1. An action of your government is shown in a fundamentally positive light when it should be shown in a more objective, or even negative, light given the circumstances.

2. Negative actions of your government are downplayed when they should be highlighted (due to their implications).

Think for Yourself 14: Identifying Stories That Favor Business Interests (for the relevant content, refer to pages 61–62)

Identify a news story in which business interests are favored over the interests of the people (or the environment) and, yet, the media fail to highlight this fact in the story.

Think for Yourself 15: Analyzing News Outlets for Similarities and Differences (for the relevant content, refer to page 62)

For any given day, closely study three mainstream news websites. Then analyze them to see how they differ and how they are similar (focusing on the homepage). Consider these questions:

1. To what extent do the three sources cover the same national news?
2. To what extent do they cover the same international news?
3. To what extent do they cover the same stories in the same or a similar way (in terms of the placement and slant of each story)?
4. After completing your analysis, what do you conclude about how mainstream news companies cover the news in your country?

Think for Yourself 16: Identifying Sensationalism in the News (for the relevant content, refer to pages 62–63)

Identify a news story in which some behavior is sensationalized. You are looking for a story that is blown out of proportion in terms of importance (while other important stories are ignored). This is easy to find in gossipy news outlets, but what about mainstream news outlets?

Think for Yourself 17: Rewrite a News Story (for the relevant content, refer to page 63–64)

Using a primary news outlet, choose a story you think you can rewrite from another viewpoint.

Rewrite the story. Explain the changes you have made and why you have made them.

Think for Yourself 18: Identifying Ignored and Important Stories
(for the relevant content, refer to page 66)

Identify a buried, underreported, or ignored story in the mainstream media news. You can look for this story either in a mainstream or an alternative news source. Summarize the story, with relevant quotes, and add your analysis. The more skilled you are at finding such stories, the better you will be able to analyze the news critically.

Think for Yourself 19: Can the Media Reform? (for the relevant content, refer to page 73)

Do you agree with our analysis that it doesn't seem possible for the news media to reform itself at present, given current conditions and the fact that most people do not think critically about the news?

Think for Yourself 20: Imagining a Critical Society and Its Implications
(for the relevant content, refer to pages 74–75)

What are some of the ways your life would probably have been different, had you been raised in a critical society? What are some of the realities we face, given that people in the world are largely irrational?

APPENDIX B

AN ABBREVIATED GLOSSARY OF CRITICAL THINKING CONCEPTS AND TERMS

critical thinking: Self-directed, self-disciplined, self-monitored, and self-corrective thinking. It presupposes assent to rigorous standards of excellence and mindful command of their use. It entails effective communication and problem-solving abilities and a commitment to overcome our native egocentrism and sociocentrism. Everybody thinks; it is our nature to do so. But much of our thinking, left to itself, is biased, distorted, partial, uninformed, or downright prejudiced. Shoddy thinking is costly, both in money and in quality of life. Excellence in thought through critical thinking must be systematically cultivated. A well-cultivated critical thinker raises vital questions and problems, formulating them clearly and precisely; gathers and assesses relevant information, using abstract ideas to interpret it effectively; comes to well-reasoned conclusions and solutions, testing them against relevant criteria and standards; thinks open-mindedly within alternative systems of thought, recognizing and assessing, as need be, their assumptions, implications, and consequences; and communicates effectively with others in figuring out solutions to complex problems.

cultural assumption: An unassessed (often implicit) belief adopted by virtue of enculturation. Raised in a society, we unconsciously take on its point of view, values, beliefs, and practices. At the root of each of these are many assumptions. Not knowing that we perceive, conceive, think, and experience within assumptions we have taken in, we take ourselves to be perceiving "things as they are," not "things as they appear from a cultural vantage point." Becoming aware of our cultural assumptions so that we critically examine them is a crucial dimension of critical thinking.

data: Facts, figures, and information from which conclusions can be inferred, or upon which interpretations or theories can be based. As critical thinkers, we must make certain to distinguish hard data from the inferences or conclusions we draw from them.

egocentrism: A tendency to view everything in relationship to oneself; to confuse immediate perception (how things seem) with reality; the tendency to be self-centered or to consider only oneself and one's own interests; selfishness. One's desires, values, and beliefs (seeming to be self-evidently correct, or superior to those of others) are often uncritically used as the norm of all judgment and experience. Egocentrism is one of the fundamental impediments to critical thinking. As one learns to think critically, one learns to become more rational, and less egocentric.

ethnocentrism: A tendency to view one's own race or culture as privileged, based on the deep-seated belief that one's own group is superior to all others. Ethnocentrism is a form of egocentrism extended from the self to the group. Much uncritical or selfish critical thinking is either egocentric or ethnocentric in nature. (Ethnocentrism and sociocentrism are used synonymously, for the most part, though sociocentrism is broader, relating to any social group, including, for example, sociocentrism regarding one's profession.) The cure for ethnocentrism or sociocentrism is empathic thought within the perspective of opposing groups and cultures. Such empathic thought is rarely cultivated. Instead, many give mere lip service to tolerance, but privileging the beliefs, norms, and practices of their own culture. Critical thinkers do not assume that the groups to which they belong are inherently superior to other groups. Instead, they attempt to accurately critique every viewpoint, seeking to determine its strengths and weaknesses. Their loyalty to a country is based on the principles and ideals of the country and not on uncritical loyalty to person, party, or national traditions.

fairmindedness: A cultivated disposition of mind that enables the thinker to treat all perspectives relevant to an issue in an objective manner. It implies having a consciousness of the need to treat all viewpoints alike, without reference to one's own feelings or selfish interests, or the feelings or selfish interests of one's friends, community, or nation. It implies adherence to intellectual standards without reference to one's own advantage or the advantage of one's group.

human nature: The common qualities of all human beings. People have both a primary and a secondary nature. Our primary nature is spontaneous, egocentric, and strongly prone to the formation of irrational beliefs . . . the basis for our instinctual thought. People need no training to believe what they want to believe: what serves their immediate interests, what preserves their sense of personal comfort and righteousness, what minimizes their sense of inconsistency, and what presupposes their own correctness. People need no special training to believe what those around them believe: what their parents and friends believe, what is taught to them by religious and school authorities, what is repeated often by the media, and what is commonly believed in the nation in which they are raised.

People need no training to think that those who disagree with them are wrong and probably prejudiced. People need no training to assume that their own most fundamental beliefs are self-evidently true or easily justified by evidence. People naturally and spontaneously identify with their own beliefs. They experience most disagreements as personal attacks. The resulting defensiveness interferes with their capacity to empathize with or enter into other points of view.

People need extensive and systematic practice to develop their secondary nature, their implicit capacity to function as rational persons. They need extensive and systematic practice to recognize the tendencies they have to form irrational beliefs. They need extensive practice to develop a dislike of inconsistency, an affinity for clarity, a passion to seek reasons and evidence and to be fair to points of view other than their own. People need extensive practice to recognize that they indeed have a point of view, that they live inferentially, that they do not have a direct pipeline to reality, that it is possible to have an overwhelming inner sense of the correctness of one's views and still be wrong.

intellectual autonomy: Having rational control of one's beliefs, values, and inferences. The ideal of critical thinking is to learn to think for oneself, to gain command over one's thought processes. Intellectual autonomy does not entail willfulness, stubbornness, or rebellion. It entails a commitment to analyzing and evaluating beliefs on the basis of reason and evidence, to question when it is rational to question, to believe when it is rational to believe, and to conform when it is rational to conform.

intellectual confidence or faith in reason: Assurance that in the long run one's own higher interests and those of humankind will best be served by giving the freest play to reason—by encouraging people to come to their own conclusions through a process of developing their own rational faculties; faith that (with proper encouragement and cultivation) people can learn to think for themselves, form rational viewpoints, draw reasonable conclusions, think coherently and logically, persuade each other by reason, and become reasonable, despite the deep-seated obstacles in the native character of the human mind and in society. Confidence in reason is developed through experiences in which one reasons one's way to insight, solves problems through reason, uses reason to persuade, is persuaded by reason. Confidence in reason is undermined when one is expected to accept beliefs on the sole basis of authority or social pressure.

intellectual courage: The willingness to face and fairly assess ideas, beliefs, or viewpoints to which we have not given a serious hearing, regardless of our strong negative reactions to them. This courage arises from the recognition that ideas considered dangerous or absurd are sometimes rationally justified (in whole or in part), and that conclusions or beliefs espoused by those around us or inculcated in us are sometimes false or misleading. To determine for ourselves which is which, we must not passively and uncritically accept what we have learned. Intellectual courage comes into play here, because inevitably we will come to see some truth in certain ideas considered dangerous and absurd and some distortion or falsity in certain ideas strongly held in our social group. It takes courage to be true to our own thinking in such circumstances. Examining cherished beliefs is difficult, and the penalties for nonconformity are often severe.

intellectual empathy: Understanding the need to imaginatively put oneself in the place of others to genuinely understand them. We must recognize our egocentric tendency to identify truth with our immediate perceptions or longstanding beliefs. Intellectual empathy correlates with the ability to accurately reconstruct the viewpoints and reasoning of others and to reason from premises, assumptions, and ideas other than our own. This trait also requires that we remember occasions when we were wrong, despite an intense conviction that we were right, and consider that we might be similarly deceived in a case at hand.

intellectual humility: Awareness of the limits of one's knowledge, including sensitivity to circumstances in which one's native egocentrism is likely to function self-deceptively; sensitivity to bias and prejudice in, and limitations of, one's viewpoint. Intellectual humility is based on the recognition that no one should claim more than he or she actually knows. It does not imply spinelessness or submissiveness. It implies the lack of intellectual pretentiousness, boastfulness, or conceit, combined with insight into the strengths or weaknesses of the logical foundations of one's beliefs.

intellectual integrity: Recognition of the need to be true to one's own thinking, to be consistent in the intellectual standards one applies, to hold oneself to the same rigorous standards of evidence and proof to which one holds one's antagonists, to practice what one advocates for others, and to honestly admit discrepancies and inconsistencies in one's own thought and action. This trait develops best in a supportive atmosphere in which people feel secure and free enough to honestly acknowledge their inconsistencies, and in which people can develop and share realistic ways of ameliorating them. It requires honest acknowledgment of the difficulties of achieving greater consistency.

intellectual discipline: The trait of thinking in accordance with intellectual standards, intellectual rigor, carefulness, order, and conscious control. The undisciplined thinker cannot recognize when he or she comes to unwarranted conclusions, confuses ideas, fails to consider pertinent evidence, and so on. Thus, intellectual discipline is at the very heart of becoming a critical person. It takes discipline of mind to keep oneself focused on the intellectual task at hand, to locate and carefully assess needed evidence, to systematically analyze and address questions and problems, to hold one's thinking to intellectual standards such as clarity, precision, completeness, consistency, and so on.

intellectual perseverance: Willingness and consciousness of the need to pursue intellectual insights and truths despite difficulties, obstacles, and frustrations; firm adherence to rational principles despite irrational opposition of others; a sense of the need to struggle with confusion and unsettled questions over an extended time to achieve deeper understanding or insight.

intellectual sense of justice: Willingness and consciousness of the need to entertain all viewpoints sympathetically and to assess them with the same intellectual standards, without reference to one's own feelings or vested interests, or the feelings or vested interests of one's friends, community, or nation; implies adherence to intellectual standards without reference to one's own advantage or the advantage of one's group.

interpret/interpretation: To give one's own conception of, to place in the context of one's own experience, perspective, point of view, or philosophy. Interpretations should be distinguished from the facts, the evidence, and the situation. (I may interpret someone's silence as an expression of hostility toward me. Such an interpretation may or may not be correct. I may have projected my patterns of motivation and behavior onto that person, or I may have accurately noticed this pattern in the other.) The best interpretations take the most evidence into account. Critical thinkers recognize their interpretations, distinguish them from evidence, consider alternative interpretations, and reconsider their interpretations in the light of new evidence.

multilogical (multidimensional) problems: Problems that can be analyzed and approached from more than one, often conflicting, points of view or frames of reference. For example, many ecological problems have a variety of dimensions: historical, social, economic, biological, chemical, moral, political, and so on. A person comfortable thinking through multilogical problems is comfortable thinking within multiple perspectives, in engaging in dialogical and dialectical thinking, in practicing intellectual empathy, in thinking across disciplines and domains.

multilogical thinking: Thinking that empathetically enters into, considers, and reasons within multiple points of view.

national bias: Prejudice in favor of one's country, its beliefs, traditions, practices, image, and worldview; a form of sociocentrism or ethnocentrism. It is natural, if not inevitable, for people to be favorably disposed toward the beliefs, traditions, practices, and worldview within which they were raised. Unfortunately, this favorable inclination commonly becomes a form of prejudice—a more or less rigid, irrational ego identification that significantly distorts one's view of one's own nation and the world at large. It is manifested in a tendency to mindlessly take the side of one's own government, to uncritically accept governmental accounts of the nature of disputes with other nations, to uncritically exaggerate the virtues of one's own nation while playing down the virtues of "enemy" nations.

National bias is reflected in the press and media coverage of every nation of the world. Events are included or excluded according to what appears significant within the dominant worldview of the nation and are shaped into stories to validate that view. Constructed to fit into a particular view of the world, the stories in the news are presented as neutral, objective accounts, and uncritically accepted as such because people tend to uncritically assume that their own view of things is the way things really are. To become responsible, critically thinking citizens and fairminded people, people must practice identifying national bias in the news and in their texts, and to broaden their perspective beyond that of uncritical nationalism.

point of view (perspective): Human thought is relational and selective. It is impossible to understand any person, event, or phenomenon from every vantage point simultaneously. Our purposes often control how we see things. Critical thinking requires that this fact be taken into account when analyzing and assessing thinking. This is not to say that human thought is incapable of truth and objectivity, but only that human truth, objectivity, and insight is almost always limited and partial, not total and absolute. By "reasoning within a point of view," then, we mean that inevitably our thinking has some comprehensive focus or orientation. Our thinking is focused ON something FROM some angle. We can change either what we are focused on or the angle of our focus. We often give names to the angle from which we are thinking about something. For example, we could look at something politically or scientifically, poetically or philosophically. We might look at something conservatively or liberally, religiously or secularly. We might look at something from a cultural or a financial perspective, or both. Once we understand how someone is approaching a question or topic (what their comprehensive perspective is), we are usually much better able to understand the logic of his or her thinking as an organized whole.

prejudice: A judgment, belief, opinion, point of view—favorable or unfavorable, formed before the facts are known, resistant to evidence and reason, or in disregard of facts that contradict it. Self-announced prejudice is rare. Prejudice almost always exists in obscured, rationalized, socially validated, functional forms. It enables people to sleep peacefully at night even while flagrantly abusing the rights of others. It enables people to get more of what they want, or to get it more easily. It often is sanctioned with a superabundance of pomp and self-righteousness. Unless we recognize these powerful tendencies toward selfish thought in our social institutions, even in what appear to be lofty actions and moralistic rhetoric, we will not face squarely the problem of prejudice in human thought and action. Uncritical and selfishly critical thought are often prejudiced.

self-deception: Deceiving oneself about one's true motivations, character, or identity. One possible definition of the human species is "The Self-Deceiving Animal." Self-deception is a fundamental problem in human life and the cause of much human suffering. A fundamental goal of critical thinking is to overcome self-deception through self-reflection.

social contradiction: An inconsistency between what a society preaches and what it practices. In every society there is some degree of inconsistency between its image of itself and its actual character. Social contradiction typically correlates with human self-deception on the social or cultural level. Critical thinking is essential for the recognition of inconsistencies, and recognition is essential for reform and eventual integrity.

sociocentrism: The assumption that one's own social group is inherently and self-evidently superior to all others. When a group or society sees itself as superior, and so considers its views as correct or as the only reasonable or justifiable views, and all its actions as justified, it has a tendency to presuppose this superiority in all of its thinking and, thus, to think closed-mindedly. All dissent and doubt are considered disloyal and rejected without consideration. Few people recognize the sociocentric nature of much of their thought.

vested interest: (1) Involvement in promoting personal advantage, usually at the expense of others, (2) people functioning as a group to pursue collective selfish goals and exerting influences that enables them to profit at the expense of others. Many groups that lobby Congress do so to gain money, power, and advantage for themselves by provisions in law that specially favor them. The term *vested interest* classically contrasts with the term *public interest*. A group that lobbies Congress in the public interest is not seeking to gain special advantage for a comparative few but, rather, protection for virtually all or the large majority. Preserving the quality of the air is a public interest. Building cheaper cars by including fewer safety features is a vested interest (it makes more money for car manufacturers).

REFERENCES AND RECOMMENDED READINGS

Atkins, L. (2016). *Skewed: A Critical Thinker's Guide to Media Bias*. Amherst, NY: Prometheus Books.

Barclay, D. (2018). *Fake News, Propaganda, and Plain Old Lies: How to Find Trustworthy Information in the Digital Age*. Lanham, MD: Rowman & Littlefield.

Bernays, E. (2004). *Propaganda*. New York: Ig Publishing.

Chomsky, N. (2002). *Media Control, Second Ed.: The Spectacular Achievements of Propaganda*. New York: Seven Stories Press.

Dice, M. (2011). *Big Brother: The Orwellian Nightmare Come True*. San Diego, CA: The Resistance.

Downie, L. and Kaiser, R. (2002). *The News About the News*. New York: Knopf.

Nadar, R. (2016). *Breaking Through Power: It's Easier Than We Think*. San Francisco, CA: City Lights Books.

Snow, L. (2017). *Mind, Media, and Madness: Alt Facts, Fake News, Russian Hacking, and What's Next*. n.p.: Novel Treasure Publishing.

INDEX

ABOUT THE AUTHORS

 Dr. Richard Paul was a leading proponent of critical thinking and through his work and legacy remains an international authority in the field. He founded the Center for Critical Thinking at Sonoma State University in 1980, followed by the Foundation for Critical Thinking. He developed concepts, principles, and theory essential to a robust and fairminded conception of critical thinking and authored more than 200 articles and seven books on the topic. He presented workshops to hundreds of thousands of educators over his thirty-five-year career as a leader in the critical thinking movement.

 Dr. Linda Elder is an educational psychologist who has taught both psychology and critical thinking at the college level. She has been president of the Foundation for Critical Thinking and executive director of the Center for Critical Thinking for almost twenty-five years. She has a special interest in the relation of thought and emotion, as well as the cognitive and affective. She has developed an original theory of the stages of critical thinking development. She has coauthored four books on critical thinking, as well as all twenty-three titles found in the Thinker's Guide Library.